D1712548

King Philip

AND THE WAR WITH THE COLONISTS

180894

Alvin Josephy's Biography Series of American Indians

King Philip

AND THE WAR WITH THE COLONISTS

Written by Robert Cwiklik

INTRODUCTION BY ALVIN M. JOSEPHY, JR.
ILLUSTRATED BY ROBERT L. SMITH

Silver Burdett Press

Sayville Library

Copyright © 1989 by The Kipling Press
Text copyright © 1989 by Robert Cwiklik
Introduction copyright © 1989 by Alvin M. Josephy, Jr.
Illustrations copyright © 1989 by Robert L. Smith

Project editors: Nancy Furstinger (Silver Burdett Press)
Mark Davies & Della Rowland (Kipling Press)
Designed by Mike Hortens

All rights reserved including the right of reproduction in whole or in
part in any form. Published by Silver Burdett Press, a division of
Simon & Schuster, Inc., Englewood Cliffs, New Jersey.
Manufactured in the United States of America

10 9 8 7 6 5 4 3 2 1 (Lib. ed.)
10 9 8 7 6 5 4 3 2 1 (Pbk. ed.)

Library of Congress Cataloging-in-Publication Data

Cwiklik, Robert
King Philip and the war with the colonists.

(Alvin Josephy's biography series of American Indians)
Bibliography: p. 132
Summary: Examines the life and fortunes of the
Wampanoag Indian leader who led an uprising against the
New England colonists in the seventeenth century.
1. Philip, Sachem of the Wamapanoags, d. 1676—Juvenile
literature. 2. Wampanoag Indians—Biography—Juvenile
literature. 3. King Philip's War, 1675–1676—Juvenile
literature. 4. Indians of North America—Rhode Island—
Biography—Juvenile literature. 5. Indians of North
America—Massachusetts—Biography—Juvenile literature.
    [1. Philip, Sachem of the Wampanoags, d. 1676.
2. Wampanoag Indians—Biography. 3. Indians of North
America—Biography. 4. King Philip's War, 1675–1676]
    I. Smith, Robert L. (Robert Logan), 1944–   ill.
            II. Title. III. Series.
E83.67.P54C85   1989   973.2′4   [B]   [92]   89-5952
          ISBN 0-382-09573-1 (lib. bdg.)
          ISBN 0-382-09762-9 (pbk.)

Contents

Although this book is based on real events and real people, some dialogue, a few thoughts, and several local descriptions have been reconstructed to make the story more enjoyable. It does not, however, alter the basic truth of the story we are telling.

Unless indicated otherwise, the Indian designs used throughout this book are purely decorative, and do not signify a particular tribe or nation.

COVER PORTRAIT COURTESY OF THE SHELBURNE MUSEUM, SHELBURNE, VERMONT

Introduction

For 500 years, Christopher Columbus has been hailed as the "discoverer" of America. But Columbus only discovered America for his fellow Europeans, who did not know of its existence. America was really discovered more than 10,000 years before the time of Columbus by people who came across the Bering Strait from Siberia into Alaska. From there they spread south to populate both North and South America. By the time of Columbus, in fact, there were millions of descendants of the true discoverers of America living in all parts of the Western Hemisphere. They inhabited the territory from the northern shores of Alaska and Canada to the southern tip of South America. In what is now the United States, hundreds of tribes, large and small, covered the land from Maine and

CREE

CANADA

NOOTKA

BLACKFOOT

CHINOOK

TILLAMOOK

SIUSLAW

WA

YAKIMA

FLATHEAD

COLUMBIA RIVER

WALLA WALLA

NEZ PERCE

GROS VENTRE

HIDATSA

MT

OR

ID

CROW

MANDAN

ND

SIOUX

TOLOWA

SHASTA

YUROK

POMO

MAIDU

WASHO

MIWOK

COSTANOA

YOKUTS

SALINA

NV

SHOSHONI

BANNOCK

WY

ARIKARA

SD

MISSOURI RIVER

CHEYENNE

PONCA

UT

ARAPAHO

NE

OMAHA

PAWNEE

PAIUTE

UTE

CO

CA

KANSAS

KS

CAHUILLA

NAVAJO

MOJAVE

HOPI

NM

KIOWA

YUMA

ZUNI

OK

AZ

PUEBLO

COMANCHE

WITCHITA

PACIFIC

PIMA

APACHE

TX

OCEAN

MEXICO

TONKAWA

RIO GRANDE RIVER

Map of
Continental United States
American Indians

MAP BY JIM ROBINSON

OJIBWA
(CHIPPEWA)

MICMAC

ALGONQUIN

ST. LAWRENCE RIVER

MENOMINEE

OTTOWA

Lake Superior

ME

MAHICAN

VT

NH

MN

WI

SAUX

MI

Lake Michigan

Lake Huron

HURON

Lake Ontario

MOHAWK

IROQUOIS

MA

MASSACHUSET

FOX

WINNEBAGO

NEUTRAL

ONONDAGA

SENECA

CAYUGA

RI

WAMPANOAG

KICKAPOO

POTAWATOMI

Lake Erie

ONEIDA

NY

CT

NARRAGANSET

PEQUOT

IA

ERIE

SUSQUEHANNOCK

DELAWARE

MOHICAN

IOWA

IL

MIAMI

PA

NJ

MISSOURI

ILLINOIS

IN

OH

MD

DE

ATLANTIC

MO

SHAWNEE

WV

VA

OSAGE

OHIO RIVER

KY

POWAHATAN

OCEAN

TN

TUSCARORA

QUAPAW

CHICKASAW

CHEROKEE

NC

AR

MISSISSIPPI RIVER

MS

AL

CATAWBA

SC

CADDO

TUNICA

GA

CREEK

N

W E

S

LA

CHOCTAW

YAMASEE

BILOXI

NATCHEZ

0   100   200   300   400   500

ATATKAPA

APALACHEE

TIMUCUA

SCALE IN MILES

GULF OF MEXICO

FL

SEMINOLE

1X

Florida to Puget Sound and California. Each tribe had a long and proud history of its own. America was hardly an "unknown world," an "unexplored wilderness"—except to the Europeans who gazed for the first time upon its forests and rivers, its prairies and mountains.

From the very beginning, the newcomers from Europe had many mistaken notions about the people whose ancestors had been living in America for centuries. At first Columbus thought he had reached the East Indies of Asia, and he called the people Indians. The name took hold and remains to this day. But there were more serious misconceptions that had a tragic effect on relations between the Indians and the Europeans. These misconceptions led to one of the greatest holocausts in world history. Indians were robbed of their possessions, their lands, and the lives of countless numbers of their people.

Most Europeans never really understood the thinking, beliefs, values, or religions of the Indians. The Indian way of life was so different from that of the Europeans, who had inherited thousands of years of diverse backgrounds, religions, and ways of thinking and acting. The Europeans looked down on the Indians as strange and different, and therefore inferior. They were ignorant in the way they treated the Indians. To the white people, the Indians were "savages" and "barbarians," who either had to change their ways and become completely like the Europeans or be destroyed.

At the same time, many Europeans came as conquerors. They wanted the Indians' lands and the resources of those lands—resources such as gold, silver, and furs. Their greed, their superior weapons, and their contempt for the Indians' "inferior" ways led to many wars. Of course the Indians fought back to protect the lives of their people, their lands, their religions, their freedoms, their very way of life. But the Europeans—and then their American descendants—assumed that the Indians were all fierce warriors who fought simply because they loved to fight. Only in recent years have we come to see the Indians as they really are—people who would fight when their lives and freedom were at stake. People who were fun-loving children, young lovers, mothers who cried for the safety and health of their families, fathers who did their best to provide food, wise old people who gave advice, religious leaders, philosophers, statesmen, artists, musicians, storytellers, makers of crafts. Yes, and scientists, engineers, and builders of cities as well. The Indian civilizations in Mexico and Peru were among the most advanced the world has ever known.

This book gets beneath the surface of the old, worn-out fables to tell a real story of the Indians—to help us understand how the Indians looked at the world. When we understand this, we can see not only what they did, but why they did it. Everything here is accurate history, and it is an exciting story. And it is told in such a way that we, the readers, can imagine ourselves back among the Indians of the past, identifying ourselves with their ways of life, beliefs, and destinies. Perhaps in the end we will be able to ask: What choices would we have had? How would we ourselves have responded and behaved?

The story told in this book took place a long time ago, very soon after the Pilgrims and Puritans first came to settle in New England. It is a story of how a lack of understanding and a series of errors led so early in our history to brutal war between the Indian tribes and the newly arrived people from Europe.

In his day, King Philip was regarded by white people as an evil man, serving the purposes of Satan against the New England settlers. But when we come to understand the Indians' side of things, we can appreciate that Philip, instead, was actually a patriot among his people. Pushed to the limit, he was trying desperately to preserve their lives, their lands, their dignity, and honor as free men and women.

—Alvin M. Josephy, Jr.

Should Old Acquaintance Be Forgot

Everyone today knows the story of the first Thanksgiving:

The Pilgrims' ship landed on the shores of North America, at Plymouth Colony, in November 1620, after a grueling sea voyage from England. Soon the cold gusts of winter kicked up. Before the Pilgrims could gather much food, snows blanketed their New England seaside settlement and the wind blew the waters of the bay cold and choppy.

Within weeks the Pilgrims had emptied the pantries on their ship, the *Mayflower*, which now lay beached on its side, lapped by the cold bay waters. The settlers huddled together in drafty seaside huts and succumbed slowly to malnutrition and overexposure to the wet, icy winds. One by one they caught fevers and chills, and one by one they died.

The survivors grew steadily paler and thinner, without a flicker of hope in their sunken, staring eyes.

By winter's end, half of the Pilgrims were dead. Then the frozen ground thawed and the moist odor of spring wafted through the settlement. It was time for planting, but the weary, starving settlers could barely lift their hoes, much less find and break good soil for farming.

One day, dark-skinned men, wearing only deerskins wrapped around their waists, appeared in the ragged colony. "Savages," exclaimed the wide-eyed Pilgrims. They had heard stories about these people in England, where they were called "Indians."

The hale and strong visitors were from the nearby tribe of Wampanoags. As soon as they saw the pale, half-starved Pilgrims, they knew what must be done. The Wampanoags' friendly chief, Massasoit, brought the settlers sacks of vegetables and slabs of meat. Massasoit's people gave them seeds and showed them the richest soil for planting, and took them to the places where the deer ran in packs, for easy hunting.

Soon the colonists' fields sprouted with green stalks of corn, peas, and squash that grew fast and tall under the summer sun. They also bagged plenty of deer for meat and even found the strength to build good, strong homes to protect them from the bitter winds of winter.

In early December 1621, the Pilgrims held a banquet with the Indians. This feast came to be known as the first Thanksgiving. Chief Massasoit, dressed in a coat of colorful feathers, warmed the chill afternoon with his constant smile. His people, clad in animal skins, sat around the table scraping food out of bowls with their hands. The prim Pilgrims, in starched chin-high collars and lofty pointed hats, winced to see such coarse table manners. But their hearts were full of tenderness for the gentle, friendly Indians who had shared everything they had. "The Lord works in mysterious ways," they mused, bowing their heads and giving thanks to God.

* * *

That much of the saga of Thanksgiving is familiar. But it's only part of the story, which ends a little over fifty years later:

In 1676, some time after the death of Chief Massasoit, many of his people were back in Plymouth. Plymouth soldiers had killed a band of Wampanoags and cut off their heads. They carried the bloody heads back to Plymouth and rammed poles into them. Then they planted the poles in a line in front of the red brick town meeting house. At the center of the grisly group stood the dripping head of Massasoit's son, known to the colonists as King Philip. His lifeless face still showed traces of the rage and pride the settlers so hated and feared.

In front of the ghastly garden of heads stood a wooden cage. Behind its thick iron bars, a naked woman and young boy cowered in the shadows, their arms and legs bound in chains.

These were the wife and son of Philip. As they stared out between the bars, Philip's blank, blind eyes stared back.

Inside the brick meeting house a group of preachers, the leaders of this religious colony, met to decide the fate of the prisoners. The preachers, dressed in flowing black robes and starched white collars, were seated around a polished oak table. The Reverend John Cotton, a grave-looking young man, opened his Bible to a page marked with string and said:

"Gentlemen, we find in the scriptures that Saul, Achan, and Haman were cut off by the Sword of Justice for the sins of their fathers. I therefore vote death to the child and its mother."

The men nodded to one another, gravely.

Then, one by one, each quoted another piece of Holy Writ.

"Gentlemen, Psalm 137 says: 'Happy shall he be, that taketh and dasheth thy little ones against the stones,'" one read.

The men nodded again. Soon all the preachers had voted death to the boy and his mother except one, who had yet to speak. The Reverend James Bridgewater, a stout man with ruddy cheeks, stood and opened his Bible.

"Gentlemen, Deuteronomy, Chapter 24: Verse 16, doth sway much with me," he said. He put his finger on the page, and read in a clear voice, "'. . . neither shall the children be put to death for the father's sins: Every man shall be put to death for his own sin.'"

The men were silent for a moment. Then they began to nod again.

It was finally decided that Reverend Bridgewater was right. They would show mercy. The boy and his mother would not be killed—merely sold into slavery.

Within the hour, Philip's wife and son were standing on the slave block at the pier. A swarthy captain of a trading ship bought them at a bargain and chained them in the dark hold of his ship. Soon they were sailing for the West Indies islands, where they would spend the rest of their lives working from fifteen to twenty hours a day under the hot tropical sun, and feeling the lash of the overseer's whip on their backs.

The preachers, their frocks blowing in the stiff bay breeze, watched the slave ship sail into the mists. Their fathers had once blessed and praised good Chief Massasoit. But now the preachers had beheaded the chief's son and sold his grandson and the boy's mother on the slave block. Obviously, something had gone very wrong since the gathering of Pilgrims and Indians at the first Thanksgiving dinner.

2

The Indian States of America

To understand what went wrong between the Pilgrims and the Indians, one must look back to a time long before the *Mayflower* carried early English settlers to the shores of North America, and even before Christopher Columbus sailed to the "New World" in 1492.

Those years prior to 1492 are often called the years before Columbus "discovered" America. But America actually was discovered more than 10,000 years earlier, by bands of Asian nomads who had crossed into North America walking, little by little, from Siberia to Alaska. Nowadays, a sea separates these two places. But at that time the sea was frozen solid, so these early American hunters and food-gatherers could live on top of it during the long hike across.

These people gradually traveled south and east, following game herds and searching for edible plants and nuts, until they populated the whole of North and South America. By the time Columbus arrived, thousands of years later, there were, some say, up to 120 million people on the American continents, with most of them in the warmer southern climates of Mexico and Central and South America. Europe during the same era had fewer than 80 million people.

When Columbus arrived, he thought he had reached the islands off the east coast of India, so he named the people of America "Indians." Of course, these bands, tribes, and chiefdoms of people had names of their own before Columbus arrived. Reading these names is often like reading the place names on a modern map of North America: the Massachusetts and Narragansett tribes of the northeast; the Cherokee, Alabama, and Biloxi tribes, farther south; the Miami, Illinois, Iowa, Wichita, Missouri, and Dakota tribes to the west, as well as hundreds of others.

Europeans looked down on the Indians and thought of them as primitive because they dressed in animal skins, lived in dirt-floor grass huts, and danced and sang in rituals that were strange to the newcomers' eyes. The "primitive" Indians, however, had done things even the "advanced" Europeans would wish to copy. For example, their farming was highly developed, and they grew many crops that had never been heard of in Europe, such as maize (called corn by Europeans), squash, tomatoes, succotash, peanuts, tobacco, chocolate, and cotton. They also produced by-products such as popcorn and chewing gum.

Modern doctors have claimed that Indian childbirth practices were better than those used by Europeans. Indian medicine men developed over 200 remedies that have since been

listed in the *Pharmacopeia of the United States* (a book listing drugs and medicinal products). An Indian cure for scurvy led to the modern discovery of the drug insulin, now used to treat diabetes. Indians used foxglove as a heart stimulant centuries before digitalis was discovered in England for the same use.

Indians thus were thriving in North and South America long before European explorers arrived. While historians now realize it is wrong to speak of Columbus "discovering" America, he and other European explorers did manage to change history in a way that is not often spoken about. In actuality, rather than discovering America, the Europeans infected it.

From the time Columbus' tall ships first hypnotized the native tribes of the Caribbean with their size and wondrous cargoes of guns, steel knives, and "far-seeing" telescopes, they also brought with them an invisible cargo that was to have a more sweeping effect than any other—disease. The sailors on these ships were carriers of smallpox, typhus, and many other infectious diseases which, centuries earlier, had wiped out millions in Europe. Over time Europeans had developed immunity to these diseases. But when the Indians were exposed, they reacted as Europeans first had—they became miserably sick and died, in vast numbers.

The effects of disease were quick and widespread. In less than a century, the population of central Mexico shrank from approximately twenty-five million to under two million. During this period, it was the same throughout South America, where roughly ninety percent of the people died of plagues.

There were fewer people in North America, perhaps ten to twelve million, but they died at a similar rate. By the end of the sixteenth century, some 500 trading ships a year had visited the coasts of North America, bringing new goods and new doses of disease and death. Some of the Europeans, however, did notice their effects on the Indians. One ship's captain, in 1585, found the Carolina Algonquians to be "marvelously wasted . . ." Their forests, where thousands of Indians once hunted and farmed, were "left desolate." In 1588 the English scientist Thomas Hariot also noticed that after white men visited Indian towns, "the people began to die very fast." Before the greatest waves of European settlers had even boarded their ships for America, the native peoples of America were dying off from infections spread by the earliest explorers from Europe.

When Massasoit became *sachem*, or chief, of the Wampanoags, the Indians in his part of the country were suffering from plagues as well. In 1615 an English slave ship, captained by Thomas Hunt, visited a Wampanoag town on the coast of what would become New England. The town was called Pawtuxet by the Indians. Hunt stopped there long enough to barter with some of the Indians and to kidnap a few others, to be sold into slavery. Less than a year later, a full-scale plague broke out in Pawtuxet and spread throughout the countryside. At one time, English traders used to see Indian campfires burning at night all along the coasts crowded with Indians. Now the fires were going out.

Massasoit could not avoid the misery and despair brought to his people by the disease. People too weak to work the fields or hunt lay day after day huddled under blankets in their huts. Everywhere was heard the low, plaintive moaning of hopeless suffering. The medicine men could do nothing—even they died. The plague struck young and old alike. Every day brought a new pile of corpses for burial. One Englishman said Indians were dying "in heaps."

All New England tribes were affected. The Pequots of southeastern Connecticut, who could once raise an army of 4,000 warriors, eventually had only 300 fighting men left. The Narragansett warriors dwindled from 5,000 to 1,000. The Massachusetts to the north "melted away," according to one observer, from roughly 10,000 people to around 1,000.

The Wampanoags were hit hardest in Pawtuxet. So many were sick in the seacoast town that Massasoit forbade his people to go there, for fear that the "witchcraft" of the great sickness would spread to all his people.

By 1620, just before the first rush of Europeans came to settle permanently in New England, every Indian in Pawtuxet had died. It was a ghost town. Its huts and fields stood empty, littered with the bleached bones of the people who had once lived there.

"Come Over and Help Us"

Shortly after the *Mayflower* landed at Paw-tuxet, renamed Plymouth by the English, the Pilgrims explored the deserted beaches and abandoned wigwams. When they found the bleached bones of the dead, they raised their eyes to heaven and thanked God for clearing the town of Indians. The mass deaths were seen as a sign of God's "wondrous wisdom and love." When King James of England got word, he quickly told his subjects about the "wonderful plague."

The Pilgrims moved into the deserted wigwams. However, only half of them were able to survive that first hard winter.

Squanto, a new member of the Wampanoag tribe, peeked into the Pilgrim settlement one morning in the spring of 1621. He saw a look of hunger and despair in the listless faces of the people. A young boy spotted Squanto, who wore only a simple buckskin draped across his hips. The boy tugged his mother's arm and pointed at the Indian. "Mama, what's that?" the boy asked.

The woman was startled. "Why, it's a savage heathen, boy. We have heard of such folk in England." The woman got the attention of one of the colony's men, who, seeing Squanto, raised his musket. The boy's eyes were wide as he stared at the tall Indian, whose bare back rippled with taut muscles. "What is a 'savage'?" he asked.

"They are creatures, half-man, half-beast," his mother answered, "whom the devil has herded into this distant wilderness, so that they will never hear the message of Christ, our Lord, and never be saved."

Squanto walked a little nearer. The scared boy grasped his mother's hand tightly.

"Courage, child," his mother said, making sure the man's gun was still trained on the Indian. "We have a duty to the Lord to bring these savages into his flock, if we can," she told the trembling boy.

Squanto walked a little closer. The man cocked his musket. The boy gripped his mother's sweaty hand. Squanto stared down the barrel of the gun. His face blossomed in a toothy smile. "Greetings, English," he said.

The Pilgrims were shocked to hear their own language coming from the mouth of this "savage." They didn't know Squanto was one of the Indians sold into slavery by a Captain Hunt a few years earlier. Squanto escaped and made his way home, first stopping in England, where he learned some English and saw the eye-popping city of London, with its huge houses and cathedrals, its harbors filled with tall ships.

The settlers soon learned to trust Squanto. He showed them the Pawtuxans' fields, cleared and ready for planting. He gave them seeds of corn and other vegetables that grew well in New England soil. He showed them places along the beach to dig in the sand for clams, and places to hunt and fish.

The other Wampanoags, even their chief, Massasoit, were no less cordial. Squanto spoke with Massasoit in his wigwam at Montaup, near present-day Bristol, Rhode Island. The chief was mourning the many deaths among his people caused by the recent plague. It made him fear for their safety. Other tribes were also suffering from plagues. During such times, tribes often made war on neighboring tribes to steal their women, in the hopes of breeding new warriors. The Narragansetts to the south especially worried Massasoit. He felt their leader was unstable and might invade at any time.

When Massasoit heard Squanto's tales of the great English king in the mighty city of London, he felt Englishmen would make good allies. With them on his side, the other tribes would fear him too much to break the peace.

Massasoit met with John Carver, the governor of Plymouth Colony. The chief was dressed in simple animal skins and moccasins. He also wore a necklace of bone and streaks of black paint on his face. Governor Carver, a grave-looking man in high collar and hat, kissed Massasoit's hand in greeting, as he would a king's.

The men sat down to talk, with Squanto as interpreter. They agreed their people should live in peace and protect one another from their enemies, and should leave their weapons home when visiting one another. Governor Carver smiled and said to Massasoit, "Our sovereign, King James I, will esteem you as his great friend and ally in the future." Massasoit smiled and grasped Governor Carver's hand. The two parted the best of friends.

Governor John Carver accepts Massasoit's peace pipe

Then the great first Thanksgiving feast was held. The tables were crowded with so much good food and drink that the feast lasted three days in all, and ushered in an era of friendship and good feeling between the Pilgrims and the Wampanoags. The Wampanoags provided Plymouth Colony the land it needed. The colonists, with their muskets and men in armor, made other Indians think twice about attacking the Wampanoags, friends of the powerful King James of England.

Soon new groups of settlers poured in from England. Some went to Plymouth Colony. Others started new colonies. In 1730 English Puritans landed in Boston harbor and started the colony of Massachusetts, named after the local Indians there. Later, more Puritans came over and settled farther south, eventually forming Connecticut.

The Puritans had broken away from the Christian Church of England in order to form a more "pure" kind of Christianity. They had much in common with the Pilgrims of Plymouth. They wanted to erect a "shining city on a hill" in America, where their new religion—and a whole new way of life—would be practiced.

The New England settlers also shared another belief—that Indians were savage, godless heathens, who must be turned into civilized, God-fearing men. Many felt the task would be easy. Indians would soon find that English shirts, pants, and dresses were better than Indian animal skins. The settlers also thought that Indians would see that English brick and stone houses, wood floors and roofs, were better than Indian thatched grass huts and dirt floors.

The colonists really believed Indians would soon be coming to them asking to be taught ways to better themselves. The colonists were ready to try to teach them.

The Massachusetts Bay Colony spelled out its mission. The colony printed a picture of a docile Indian on its colonial seal, with the plea "Come over and help us" issuing from the Indian's lips. This seal was stamped on advertisements that were handed around England to attract people to the new colony.

For many years, the Wampanoags and their new English neighbors lived in peace and good will, freely visiting each other in their villages. Indians and colonists joined in dancing and singing parties, and could be seen traipsing to one another's homes to "cut a cantico," as the expression went.

But something puzzled the colonists. The Indians visited Englishmen daily. They had a firsthand opportunity to observe the "superior" qualities of English life. Yet they seemed content to live the way they always had.

The Indians did, however, show a great appetite for English goods: wool blankets, steelhead axes, scissors and needles, and

The Colonial seal

guns for hunting. Some even began to wear English fashions, usually ragged castoffs, which made them look like forest vagabonds. But most Indians still showed no desire to live like Englishmen, which is what the Englishmen wanted. Most of them still wore only animal skins, and preferred life in their thatched huts in the forest to the orderly brick and stone homes of Plymouth and Boston.

The Englishmen were put off by the Indians' stubbornness. But they consoled themselves. Perhaps the Indians merely needed more time, more exposure to Englishmen.

In years to come, Indians had no shortage of exposure to Englishmen. So many boatloads of settlers poured into the colonies that the colonists began to call the area "New England." During this time, as the colonies' population grew, the Indians' population continued to shrink from diseases. By around 1635 the Massachusetts Bay Colony alone numbered 17,000 people, far more than the dwindling Massachusetts Indians, whose population had dipped to less than 1,000 and was still dropping.

Chief Massasoit could not help but notice his country had changed dramatically in the fifteen years since the first Thanksgiving dinner with the colonists. He was concerned that the English were growing a little too powerful. But he was also relieved. The chiefs of the Narragansetts and other nearby tribes knew that the Wampanoag sachem was a friend of the English king. As the power of the English grew, the power of Massasoit grew with it. Though Massasoit kept calm about English expansion, something happened in the year 1637 to give him and all the Indians of the area a scare.

Not all tribes were as friendly with the English as were the Wampanoags. The Pequots, a tribe in Connecticut, had been feuding with the Puritans for some years over their trading rights. The feuds were usually settled in a friendly way, but one turned into a bloody massacre. In the spring of 1637, Massachusetts and Connecticut militiamen were sent to "take care of" the Pequots.

The Pequots understood that the English meant to make war. In those days, Indians had many customs about warfare between tribes. For one thing, women and children were not to be harmed. Indian wars were not very violent in any case. Often, battles were brief, with only a few men injured. But to injure a woman or a child in combat was considered cowardly by Indians.

The Pequots wondered how the English felt about this custom. During an early skirmish, a Pequot chief asked the English commander, "Do you English kill women and children?" The commander replied, "You shall see that hereafter." It was not very reassuring.

So the Pequots sent their women and children to a fort at Mystic, on the Thames River, to keep them out of the fighting. The Pequot warriors, meanwhile, were in another fort some miles down the road, waiting for the attack of the militia. Though the English outnumbered them, the Indians were ready to stand and fight.

But the English commander avoided the warriors at the main fort. Instead, he marched for Mystic, with the sole intention of attacking their women and children. The English were traveling with bands of Narragansett and Mohegan Indians, who had agreed to help punish the Pequots. Many of these deserted when they realized the English plan meant that women and children would be killed.

Just before dawn, the English surrounded Mystic with two rings of soldiers. Shortly after the first light, the soldiers started firing at anything that moved. Mothers and the wailing babies in their arms were shot. Old men and women, hobbling in panic, were pitilessly gored. Naked little children ran screaming, headlong into the dripping blades of the English. The soldiers lobbed flaming torches atop the wigwams, and the town was turned into a roaring furnace. An Englishman later wrote that many of the Pequots "were broiled" in the flames. Between 400 and 700 Pequots were massacred. Only two Englishmen were killed.

Captain Mason, who masterminded the attack, later wrote, ". . . should not Christians have more mercy and compassion?" Mason answered his own question by appealing to the Bible. "Sometimes, the Scriptures declareth . . . children must perish with their parents," he said.

The Englishmen's Indian helpers were now ashamed of what they had seen. They screamed at the English that their wicked method of fighting was "too furious, and slays too many . . . "

To justify what they had done, the English began to talk about Indians as if they weren't really human beings. They had always thought Indians were "children of the devil." Now they openly discussed Indians' so-called savage ways. The Puritans seemed to think that, since Indians were "less than human," to massacre them was all right.

To the Indians, it was the English who had behaved as less than humans. Indians saw a new side of the white men who had so quickly flooded their country, and they didn't like what they saw.

Soon after the attack on Mystic, English troops cornered the heartbroken Pequot warriors and killed almost all of them. John Winthrop, governor of Massachusetts Colony, wrote a letter to William Bradford of Plymouth about the Pequot massacre. Winthrop reported, "Our people are all in health (the Lord be praised) and although they had marched . . . all the day and had been in fight all the night they . . . found themselves so fresh as they could willingly have gone to such another business." In other words, they felt "fresh" enough to do the whole thing over again.

Governor Winthrop held the letter before him and blew the ink dry. Then he took the seal of his colony and stamped it onto the document. The waxy image of the docile Indian could scarcely be seen, and his silent cry, "Come over and help us," barely remembered.

4
Where the Light Rises

Massasoit awoke to the sound of crying. He looked around the dark wigwam. His wife and infant son were still asleep on the bearskin blanket. Massasoit got up to look outside. Two women and a little boy cowered in the flickering light of a torch held by a sleepy Wampanoag brave. Their sobbing, sweaty faces were covered with soot.

"They have killed all . . . the white men have killed all," the women wailed, gasping for air.

Massasoit knelt next to them and listened to their story. The women were Pequots, some of the lucky ones who had escaped the Englishmen in Connecticut. They lifted their tear-streaked faces to the chief. "What kind of war is it, that destroys all, even the families?" the women sobbed.

The gentle Massasoit felt his own eyes fill with tears as he listened to the horrible story of the massacre. Could it be true that white soldiers behaved in this way? One glance at the fear in the eyes of these people told Massasoit that it was true. But why? Massasoit told the brave to give shelter to the refugees. The chief returned, troubled, to his wigwam.

Around Massasoit's home town of Montaup that night, the glow of firelight spread from wigwam to wigwam as word of the massacre circulated. Massasoit tossed the rest of the night. He was heartsick. But he comforted himself with the thought that at least the men of Plymouth were not involved.

Massasoit looked over at his wife and their infant son, Wamsutta, cradled in her arms. Wamsutta would be chief himself one day. Massasoit's wife was expecting another child soon. He suddenly imagined English soldiers attacking his town, killing his family, his wife and son—the unborn child. The chief gritted his teeth. "No," he murmured. "The Plymouth men are not so."

For many months the Pequots' tale spread to every council fire of the Northeastern tribes. It was a time of sorrow and gloomy foreboding. It was during these uneasy times that the sound of another squalling infant was heard in Massasoit's wigwam. The chief's wife bore him a second son. They named him Metacom.

Perhaps the time of Metacom's birth meant he was destined for his later role as King Philip. Until that time, the English had seemed almost godlike to the Indians. Now, after the Pequot troubles, the Indians weren't so sure. Instead of talking about the white men's wonderful magic, their wigwams buzzed with tales of white men's horrifying cruelty. It was in this new atmosphere that Metacom grew up.

Metacom's early life showed no hint of his later infamy. He spent his first months in a cradleboard, like any other Indian child. The cradleboard was made of a sleeve of deerskin attached to a board. The sleeve had holes in the top and sides, for the baby's head and arms.

Indian mothers didn't have to take time off from work when they had babies. They slung the children on their backs like backpacks. When they worked at weeding rows of corn, peas, and squash, the mothers hung the cradleboards from the branches of bushes or trees.

As Metacom learned to toddle and walk, he was allowed to play with the other children. But Indian parents didn't dress their children before they reached the age of twelve or thirteen. The sight of naked Indian children, running and playing, was common and wholesome to the Indians. But it was, regrettably, one more excuse for white men to brand Indians "savage."

When Metacom was a youngster, it was his brother, Wamsutta, who was set apart for special treatment. As the eldest male child, Wamsutta was the heir apparent to Massasoit. He would be supreme sachem of all the Wampanoags one day.

Massasoit liked to take his sons for rides in a birchbark canoe along the bay shore. As they paddled along the beach, the chief told stories about the days before the yellow sickness came.

Massasoit pointed to the shore, where a dozen men and women knelt in ankle-deep water digging in the sand for clams. "Back then, there were more diggers along the beach," the chief said. "So many, you could hardly see the sand."

Massasoit stroked the canoe through the water, still musing on the past. He pointed to the treetops beyond the beach. "Back then, there were as many women in our fields as stalks of corn, and our hunters in the forest were as numerous as the trees themselves," the chief said in a quiet, sad voice.

Massasoit watched his sons' faces. Wamsutta forced his features into a look of solemn pride, as if he were practicing to be a chief. This made Massasoit smile. But Metacom was different. The young boy seemed to grasp the words of his father and hold them in his mind for a long time. Metacom had a quiet, thoughtful way about him that his father admired.

The hilltop town of Montaup, the town in which Massasoit and his family lived, was the center of the Wampanoag community. The town lay in a peninsula—an arm of land surrounded by water on three sides. The peninsula jutted into the choppy waters of Narragansett Bay. The lands to the south and east of the peninsula, all the way to the sweeping arm of Cape Cod and the islands of Nantucket and Martha's Vineyard, were also controlled by the Wampanoags, even though their peoples had different names. To the south the people were called Sakonnets. To the east were the Pocassets. These tribes had been loyal to the Wampanoags since before anyone could remember, and they still looked to the council fire atop Montaup—the highest point in the bay area—for guidance and protection.

After they had paddled for some time, the little canoe came in sight of the islands. Massasoit pointed to the men on the shore of Martha's Vineyard, casting nets in the water for fish, quahogs (a type of large clam), and shrimp.

Metacom loved to listen to his father talk about the time before the yellow sickness, when Wampanoags filled the forests and the beaches. Metacom felt this talk was meant for Wamsutta, to teach him, to make him proud of the people he would one day lead, to make him understand how to be a chief. Still Metacom could listen, too.

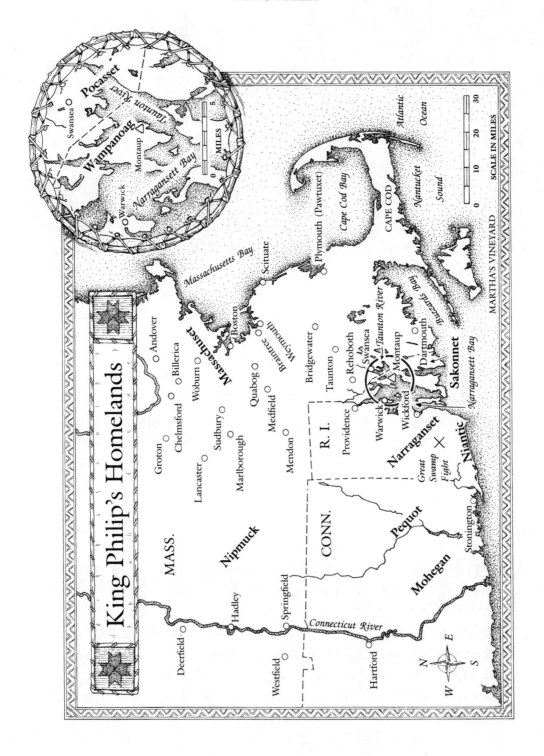

King Philip's Homelands

Metacom could not overlook the sadness in his father's voice when he talked of the old days. Standing atop Montaup, below the rosy evening sky, Massasoit would wave his arm over the vast lands the Wampanoags held in times past. "Even to the edge of the sea, where the sun rises," he said. But now Plymouth men were pushing ever farther west, and they controlled the land where the sun comes up as well.

Massasoit turned around and pointed west, across the bay, to the land of the Narragansetts. "But the white men have made things good," he said wearily. "They have kept the Narragansetts from landing on these shores and making us bow to them." Wamsutta nodded and smiled. "Yes, the white men have made things good," he said, echoing his father.

Metacom looked at his father and listened carefully. Massasoit's words said he was happy with his Plymouth allies, but his voice, strained and faint, said otherwise.

When Metacom and Wamsutta grew old enough to wear skins over their bodies like men, they were also old enough to work. One day Metacom sat down with one of the men to learn to whittle branches of sturdy oak and hickory into arrows and bows and to shape stones into arrowheads. The work required concentration, for the arrows had to be weighed and shaped to fly straight and fast, and the arrowheads had to be sharp enough to pierce an animal's tough hide.

When some Wampanoag hunters walked by and saw Metacom scratching and scraping on the sticks and stones, they laughed. One held out his musket and said, "Bah, this is the tool of the hunter." Muskets were growing more and more popular for hunting. It was easier to make lead musket balls than to make arrows, and muskets shot farther than bows. Besides, muskets gave off a loud, satisfying "crack" when fired.

Out on the hunt, Metacom was surprised the hunters didn't stop when they had shot enough game to feed and clothe the people in the town. They kept firing at the furry creatures, killing them quickly and easily, especially beavers.

Game wasn't used just to take care of the needs of the tribe any longer. English traders gave Indians goods and sometimes even silver for beaver skins and other pelts, which they made into fur coats and blankets for sale in Europe. Europeans paid high prices in silver and gold for the furs.

The English paid the Indians in wool blankets, steel knives and needles, clothing, and much-loved muskets. Indians grew so fond of English goods that they hunted for more and more skins, until the animals in the forests near Montaup began to disappear. Soon Indians had to go on long hunting trips—sometimes hiking for several days—to track down enough animals.

Other things were disappearing from the Indians' lives as well.

Evenings, after dinner, Massasoit loved to sit down by the fire with Metacom and Wamsutta to tell stories. As the boys waited, wide-eyed and anxious, the chief took his time filling and lighting his stone stag's head pipe, taking deep pulls, and blowing out big blasts of smoke. Then Massasoit stared into the flickering firelight, as if he were staring into the past itself, and told his sons of the old things.

Massasoit told them the story of how the Great Spirit, who made the Earth, created people when he saw the Earth was a lonely place without any. The Great Spirit took a stone from the ground and fashioned the first man. Then the Spirit selected a tree in the forest, from which he made the first woman. These two were the father and mother of the people who eventually became known as the Wampanoags, a name that means "people of the place where the light rises." The Wampanoags' towns had bordered the sea on the East Coast. Since the sun rises from the East, seeming to burst forth right from the water, the tribe's name had come naturally.

One evening, when Massasoit had finished telling a story, he tapped his pipe on a rock to empty it. But he tapped a little too hard, and the pipe cracked and split into two pieces. Metacom saw the sadness in his father's eyes as he picked up the two ends of his pipe and held them together. Then Wamsutta tried to cheer things up. "Don't be sad, Father, you can have another carved for you," Wamsutta said.

Massasoit stroked his chin and calmly said, "In old times, you would be right, and I may indeed be glad to break one pipe, so that I could get another. But this pipe was made by Smiling Rock, a man with magic hands, who is now dead and gone to the Happy Place in the Southwest. Since none of our young men wished to learn his magic while he was alive—they are all too busy hunting beaver skins to pay for their new muskets and English clothing—there will be no more pipes such as this one."

Stag's head pipes weren't the only things in short supply these days. The craftsmen of the tribe who carved masks for ceremonies, as well as all sorts of statuettes, poles, and pipes, sat alone in their old age. At one time young people were eager to learn the wisdom of these artisans before they died. Now young people wanted only to hunt. Without pupils to teach, the skills of the old Indian artisans died with them.

Wamsutta again tried to cheer his father. He smiled and said, "No matter, Father. You can also trade skins to the English, but for a new pipe, rather than a musket."

Massasoit said nothing. He merely stared at the stag's head in his hand, its perfectly wrought antlers and proud snout. Metacom had never cared one way or another for this pipe or his father's smoking. But now he, too, was saddened by its loss.

5

Strangers in Their Own Land

The judge, dressed in black robes and a white powdered wig, sat behind the high altar that towered over the courtroom. "Bring in the accused," he thundered.

At the back of the room, a pair of doors swung open and two bailiffs roughly escorted an Indian to the bench, each pulling him by one arm.

A half-dozen well-dressed Plymouth citizens sat in the spectators' benches, waiting to bring some business or other before the court. One of these, on seeing the barebacked Indian, quipped, "By the grace of God, I did not know there was to be a powwow in His Majesty's court today." The other spectators chuckled at the joke.

The Indian's face flushed red with anger when he heard the white men laugh. The two bailiffs stopped before the bench with the prisoner, who gritted his teeth and looked up at the judge.

"You are charged with the willful destruction of the property of a citizen of this colony," the judge proclaimed. "How do you plead?"

The Indian stood stiff and speechless. He did not understand English, so he could not possibly reply. He was not even aware the judge was talking to him.

"This savage is as guilty as Cain himself, your honor," one of the bailiffs stated. "He did destroy the pig of an honest citizen of Plymouth."

Though the bailiff spoke the truth, it was not the whole story, as he well knew. The Indian had recently found several pigs traipsing through the Indians' vegetable fields. The animals were chomping on green ears of corn and trampling over the other vegetable plants, laying waste to the entire field.

The Indian knew the animals belonged to one of the English farmers in nearby Rehoboth. The Englishmen were supposed to keep their animals fenced in so that they wouldn't wander into the Indians' fields. The Indians depended on vegetable crops for survival. It was no laughing matter. But the colonists, time and again, treated the Indians' complaints as a joke. The man gripped his musket. He would show them a joke.

The Indian ran up to the field. The pigs squealed and scurried away—all but one. That pig was too busy chomping corn to notice the Indian, who aimed his rifle and fired. With a pained squeal, the pig's corn-swiping days were ended.

In the courtroom, the judge scowled at the Indian. "Since you cannot speak for yourself and no one is available to speak for you, I must find you guilty as charged. I sentence you to ten days in the stockade and a fine of twenty shillings. Next case!" the judge's voice boomed as he pounded his gavel. The

bewildered Indian, who still had no idea what was happening, was led from the courtroom.

The Indian was taken to the jailhouse and thrown into a dark, musty cell crowded with prisoners. Now he understood. He was being punished! Punished for defending the crops of his people against the scavenging swine of the English.

A swarthy English sailor, arrested for drunkenly attacking a man with a knife, lay on the floor, his mouth wide open, snoring. A group of rumpled drunks and oily common thieves from the streets of Plymouth slumped against the walls. There were also a few other Wampanoags in a corner of the cell.

One of the drunks, a toothless, sooty-faced man, complained to the guards who brought the new prisoner. "Another Indian," he snarled. "What would the king say if he knew you were locking his subjects in with savage animals? Have you never heard of the Magna Carta?" The guards ignored the man and walked away. The man screamed, "You have no right to cage me with this . . . this animal!"

The Indian didn't understand what had been said, but he knew it wasn't friendly. He sat next to his fellow Wampanoags. He was relieved to be able to speak to someone again. "My brothers, what is it that brings you here amidst the scum of the English," he said.

The Wampanoags explained their cases. One, a middle-aged Indian with graying hair, had been caught hunting on land the English had bought from the Wampanoags a short time before. But the English and the Wampanoags understood the idea of "buying," at least when it came to land, in different ways. The Indians thought the English were only paying to "use" the land along with the Indians. The English thought they were paying for the right to own the land and keep everyone else off it.

The Indians didn't understand. Did the English mean they "owned" the land the way one owns a knife or a gun? Surely a man may have a knife or a gun to himself. But knives and guns are made by men for other men. Land is another matter. Land was made by the Great Spirit, for the use of all men. At least, that is what the Indians believed, and they failed to understand the English craving to "possess" land.

On the other hand the English did not understand the Indians' idea of "sharing" land. How can land be shared? It must either be "yours" or "ours" the English said.

The middle-aged Wampanoag hunter was convicted of trespassing and sentenced to ten days and ten shillings. Now he sat in that miserable hole of a cell, among the lowest of the low, merely for hunting on land he had hunted on for years.

When these Indians got out of jail, they had bitter feelings for the men at Plymouth. Many others grew to share those feelings as more and more Indians' fields were overrun with cattle and more were jailed for hunting on former Indian lands.

Back at Montaup, Massasoit was saddened to hear of the shabby treatment his people got at the hands of the colony and the courts. Many of his people wanted him to take action against Plymouth—to stop selling them land or even to consider breaking his treaty. But Massasoit did not want that. After all, the chief reasoned, Plymouth's leaders still showed him all the respect he was due as chief. They bowed and kissed his hand and brought him gifts. And Plymouth was still his best insurance against an attack by the Narragansetts.

But the people's complaints of unfair treatment from the colony persisted. They were upset about the white men's legal system. Englishmen arrested Indians for violations of English law, even on Indian property. Then they would not listen to Indian testimony in court, only to that of other white men. Also, Indians could seldom serve on juries.

Massasoit spoke to the Plymouth leaders about his people's grievances. The Englishmen said they would try to be more fair in legal dealings with the Indians. They also agreed to put up a fence between the colony and the Wampanoags' land, to keep animals from straying into the Indians' crops. Metacom and Wamsutta walked back to Montaup with Massasoit after the meeting. The chief was happy to have done something good for his people.

But Massasoit's pleasure was short-lived. The fence the colonists' promised was placed twenty-five miles from Plymouth, and only five miles from Montaup. The English were closing in. It no longer seemed as if the English were visitors in the Wampanoags' country. The Wampanoags began to feel like strangers in their own land.

🀩🀩🀩🀩🀩 **6** 🀩🀩🀩🀩🀩

The Chief Is Dead

The Plymouth preacher stood before his congregation in the crowded meeting house. "Brethren, I bring you sad news on this Sabbath," he said. "The noble Chief Massasoit lays gravely ill at his home on Mount Hope." Though the preacher, like all colonists, got the name of Montaup wrong, he got the message right. Massasoit was dying. It was big news to the Sunday crowd of churchgoers.

"If God can show mercy on the children of Satan, he will have mercy on this savage," the preacher said. "Amen," said the people.

Massasoit had been a good friend of the Plymouth colony ever since the Pilgrims reached Plymouth Rock in 1620, some forty-one years before. He nurtured them when they were weak.

Could the colonists expect such friendliness from the Wampanoags' next chief? They pondered this question as they filed out of church that Sunday morning.

On Montaup, a crowd of Wampanoags kept a quiet vigil outside the wigwam of their ailing chief. Inside, Wamsutta sat by his sleeping father, holding his hand and listening to the chanting of the medicine man. Beside Wamsutta sat his wife, Weetamo, chief of the Pocassets. Massasoit had arranged his son's marriage to the sachem of the Pocassets to make the bond between them and the Wampanoags unbreakable.

Metacom sat by the fire in the center of the wigwam. He looked at the frown of worry on his brother's face. Metacom was now twenty-four years old. Wamsutta, only a couple of years older, had been Metacom's closest companion all his life. But, somehow, tonight everything was changing.

Their father had been sick for many days now. As each day passed and his condition grew worse, Wamsutta became less a young man and more a chief. Now, as Massasoit neared his end, Wamsutta grew quieter, more thoughtful than ever before.

The firelight flickered in Metacom's face. As he noticed the changes in his brother, he realized his life, too, would change. Metacom knew Wamsutta would need his help. Every chief needs counselors. Metacom had never taken tribal business very seriously before. He only had time for hunting, walking through the woods, and paddling his canoe along the beaches of the bay. Could he grow old and wise now all at once and be a help to his brother?

Metacom's palms were sweaty with nervousness. How much more anxious must his brother feel? He stared at Wamsutta, whose serene expression seemed to be a mask, hiding his doubts. Would Wamsutta be a good chief? Would he deal out justice fairly? Would he use the power of life and death wisely? Would he have the strength to use the club on criminals to beat them to death for their wrongs? Most importantly, how would he handle the men of Plymouth, who every day threatened to take further advantage of the Indians?

In the middle of the night, with his weeping and weary family looking on, Massasoit died. "Let his spirit go to the Happy Place," said the medicine man, who shook his gourd rattle and sang a song for the dead.

Wampum belt

Plymouth's leading citizens came to Massasoit's funeral. Many made fine speeches, remembering the friendship Massasoit had shown to the colony at the time of the first Thanksgiving. But Metacom noticed the ones who made the fine speeches were old and gray men, now retired and near death themselves. It was the young men who now wielded the power in the colony. They had no kind words for Massasoit. These men were the same age as Wamsutta and Metacom. They did not understand the Pilgrims' grim early days in this country, when the old chief had saved the people of Plymouth. That happened before the young men of Plymouth were born.

After the funeral, Metacom seldom saw Wamsutta, who was once always by his side, walking the paths of the forests and along the bay shore. Chief Wamsutta was now too busy. Metacom went off to the forests to hunt with the other men from the tribe, but he somehow felt all alone.

Even hunting itself was not what it used to be. The fur trade had caused the forests nearby to be overhunted, and now the game was nearly wiped out. Furs were scarce. This was bad news for the Indians, who had grown accustomed to the European goods their furs bought; it would be difficult to find a way to pay for more of those goods.

Now Indians began to work on the farms of colonists, to make wages to buy English goods. But the Indians were not happy with the situation. Now that Massasoit and the lucrative fur trade were both dead and gone, the colony seemed to forget all the Indians once did for them. Plymouth farmers made the strong Indians work like oxen, while giving poor wages and little respect.

Indians were already upset with colonists for taking tribal land and ruining tribal crops with farm animals. Now the Indians had a new complaint, the mistreatment of their laborers. It seemed that relations would get worse before they got better.

Metacom met with Wamsutta to help his brother decide on a course of action. Both had sensed the same thing at their father's funeral: The men who ruled Plymouth now were too young to remember the bond their fathers had made with Massasoit and the Wampanoags. The sons of Massasoit decided it was time to renew that bond.

The next morning, Wamsutta dressed in his finest skins, decorated with strips of purple and white wampum woven in many patterns. He wore a single feather in his hair and a necklace of bone given him by his father. Metacom was also dressed in a splendid wampum vest. The two traveled to Plymouth just after first light, accompanied by a guard of twenty braves. The people of Montaup watched proudly as Wamsutta passed with his retinue, looking for all the world like a dignified chief.

The leaders of Plymouth Colony could not help snickering when they saw Wamsutta and his train of followers coming into town. "Here's the young Indian, playing like a chief," many snickered. But they greeted Wamsutta courteously.

Wamsutta told the colonists that he had come to renew the bond of friendship between their peoples. As a symbol of this new bond, he asked if the English would give him and his brother English names, a mark of affection.

The English were delighted. But they couldn't help treating Wamsutta's request as something of a joke. They quickly decided which names to give the Indians. With a wink and a nod, they gave Wamsutta the name Alexander, after the famed Macedonian world conqueror Alexander the Great. This they found amusing, for to them Wamsutta looked like anything but a world conqueror. As for Metacom, they gave him the name Philip, after Alexander the Great's father, King Philip of Macedon.

After the new names were written in the Plymouth records, Wamsutta and his retinue started home. The chief was happy he had begun to restore good feelings with his powerful allies at Plymouth. The Plymouth men, however, who had a good chuckle out of the whole thing, were pleased for another reason. They were now convinced of what they had long suspected: With Massasoit gone, they could do whatever they pleased with the Wampanoags and their land.

Meanwhile, Wamsutta grew more comfortable in his role as chief. He felt as if he were carrying things out just as his father would have done. The English had given him the name of a king, he reasoned, so they must understand that he intended to behave as one.

He soon found out how foolish he had been.

Wamsutta had a meeting with Roger Williams, the governor of the new colony of Rhode Island to the south. Williams was hated by the religious men of Plymouth,

Massachusetts, and Connecticut. He favored things those pious men thought were "scandalous" if not downright wicked. The ideas Roger Williams believed in, such as freedom of religious practice and fair treatment for all people—including Indians— were revolutionary for their day. The religious zealots of the New England colonies thought Williams was a dangerous man, and they had banished him from their lands.

Williams had made friends with many tribes of Indians, however, and they helped him start a new colony, which the reformer named Rhode Island. Williams wished to buy some land from Wamsutta for his growing colony, which was filling up with all types of religious groups, such as the Quakers, whom the prickly Puritans and Pilgrims would not tolerate. Wamsutta agreed to sell Williams the land.

When the leaders of Plymouth found out about the sale of Wampanoag land to the Rhode Island Colony, they were furious. They had long hoped the Wampanoags would only sell land to them. Now they saw they had competition, and they didn't like it. It was decided to send an emissary to Wamsutta, to persuade the new chief that selling land to anyone but the people of Plymouth was not very friendly.

The Plymouth emissary was Josiah Winslow. His father, Edmund Winslow, had been a close friend of the late Chief Massasoit, and Josiah was also closely acquainted with the family of the Wampanoag sachem. Winslow did not travel alone to visit his friends, however. He went with forty armed men.

When Winslow arrived at Wamsutta's wigwam, he found the chief lying on his back on his bearskin bed, sick with a fever. His wife, Weetamo, and the medicine man did not wish to allow the visitor to enter, but Wamsutta, recognizing the old friend of his family, waved him inside.

Wamsutta was happy to see Winslow. Years before, when

Massasoit lay gravely ill in this very wigwam, Edmund Winslow, Josiah's father, paid the chief a visit. The elder Winslow had brought the ailing chief hot soup mixed with herbs for his ills. The next day, the chief was feeling much better. He gave his good friend credit for his recovery.

Now Edmund Winslow's son approached Wamsutta and kissed the young chief's hand. He spoke in English, which both Wamsutta and his brother, Metacom, had been taught to speak in their youths. Wamsutta soon learned, however, that young Winslow was not here to feed him soup.

"We have heard of your business with Roger Williams," Winslow said. "I have come to invite you to travel with me to Duxbury, to discuss the matter with the leaders of Plymouth Colony."

Wamsutta smiled weakly. Patting Winslow's hand, he said, "I am too weak to visit my Plymouth friends now. Please, tell them I will be happy to meet with them after this moon fades, by which time my strength will surely return."

Winslow drew back his hand and said, "I'm afraid you must come with me, Wamsutta. The leaders of Plymouth Colony require your presence."

Wamsutta's relaxed and cordial manner vanished. He shot a cold stare at Winslow and said, "You say I 'must' come with you. This word 'must' cannot be spoken to a sachem," he scolded. "I will do as I choose, and I will meet with your Plymouth leaders when and if I choose to do so." Wamsutta coughed and lay his head back down.

Winslow calmly pulled out a gun and pressed it against Wamsutta's ribs. The young chief's eyes now opened wide. "If you refuse to come with me, Wamsutta, you are a dead man," Winslow said coolly.

To the Happy Place

Wamsutta felt the cold barrel of Winslow's gun against his ribs. It made his anger rise even more. "The men of Plymouth call themselves my friends, yet they invite me to visit by holding a gun at my chest," he fumed. Winslow said nothing, but he did not put down his pistol.

Weetamo and the medicine man sat by, silently, as if in shock. It was not right to give orders to a sachem. The English would never have done such a thing when Massasoit was alive. Perhaps they felt Wamsutta was less a chief. Weetamo looked into Wamsutta's eyes and said, "You must go, my husband, but you must go as a sachem goes, with your train and your honor safe."

Wamsutta was in no mood to go anywhere, but he saw he had little choice. His death would serve nothing, and it was obvious that Winslow meant to kill him if he refused. Winslow agreed that Wamsutta could travel with a full escort of men to conduct him as a sachem. But this was a mere formality. The insult had already gone too deep.

Wamsutta was carried by an escort of braves on a litter to Duxbury, where he was questioned by the leaders of Plymouth about his sales of land to Roger Williams. Wamsutta was feeling weak with his illness, but he answered the men's questions. "The land belongs to our people," Wamsutta said. "We will sell it to whomever we choose."

The colonists told Wamsutta they were disappointed. They thought Plymouth had a "special friendship" with the Wampanoags. Wamsutta smiled weakly. "If you treat your special friends as you have treated me, you will soon find that you have no friends left," he said.

The Plymouth leaders were frustrated. They could not deny that Wamsutta was right. Their treaty with Massasoit merely said the Wampanoag chief, whoever he is, is a "friend and ally" of the English king. It made no rules about how the Wampanoags could or should sell their land. They could do with it as they pleased. Plymouth's leaders had summoned Wamsutta not to make him abide by the treaty, which he had never broken, but to scare him. They wanted his people's land. Not only that, they were convinced that God wanted them to have it.

In the meantime, Wamsutta's fever seemed to be getting worse. His face was flushed and sweaty. Now it was the colonists who were scared. They didn't want Wamsutta to die as their prisoner. It would look bad in England, where it was thought Indians ought to be treated fairly.

The Plymouth leaders adjourned the meeting and sent Wamsutta back to Montaup with Winslow. But Wamsutta was in no condition to travel. Instead, he was taken to Winslow's house. Wamsutta spent one night there, and then demanded to be taken home, sick or not. He would not stay another minute in the home of the man who had held a gun to his breast.

Wamsutta's men put him atop the litter and began the long walk back to Montaup. But Wamsutta shortly grew delerious with fever. Weetamo sat next to him on the litter and placed his head in her lap. The young chief, his face beaded in sweat, smiled at his wife one last time. Then Weetamo felt Wamsutta's body shake and his life slip away. He was dead. Weetamo held his lifeless face in her hands for a long time, weeping.

The next day Metacom returned to Montaup from a long hunting trip. He sensed something was wrong at the eerily quiet hilltop town. No one was at work in the fields; no one walked to and fro among the houses. Metacom saw a large crowd of Wampanoags gathered near his brother's wigwam. When the people saw Metacom, he was surrounded by his brother's bodyguards and led off to the tent. "What is it?" Metacom asked.

"You are sachem now," one of the guards answered. "Your brother has gone to the Happy Place."

The guards led the stunned Metacom into the wigwam, where he found Weetamo and his younger brother and sisters, their eyes red from weeping. They rushed to Metacom, but he walked past them to his brother's body, stretched stiff and lifeless on the bearskin.

When Metacom saw his brother's face, its features frozen in death, tears flooded his eyes. He turned to Weetamo. "Why? He was in health when I went away."

Weetamo asked the others to leave the wigwam. She

explained what had happened between Winslow and Wamsutta. Metacom paced back and forth in the tent, his fists balled up at his sides. "They have killed my brother," he muttered. "They have killed my chief."

Metacom turned sullen. He sulked the rest of the day, staring into the fire for hours, speaking to no one. When evening came, he walked outside, past his guards, past the houses in the village, toward the forest. The people watched him pass. He ignored their stares. He had not yet begun to think about the fact that he was their chief now—the sachem of the Wampanoags. He could not think of anything except the question: Why?

Metacom walked the trails to the place high in the hills where he and Weetamo often went with Massasoit. He stood on the high hilltop below the misty twilight sky and looked out at the crashing bay waters to the south. He took a deep breath of the tangy salt air, scanning the marshlands and forests to the east. Then he thought he heard his father's voice telling Wamsutta, "As far as you can see are your lands and your people."

Now, both Massasoit and Wamsutta were gone. But the people were still out there, and they still looked to this high hill for leadership and protection.

Metacom scanned the northeast, where the border with the Plymouth settlements lay. Hot tears streaked his face. Before he could stop himself, he took a deep breath and screamed:

"Why . . . ?"

Metacom beat his chest with his fists and screamed over and over, "Why? . . . Why? . . . Why?"

He sighed and lowered his arms to his sides. Then he stood quietly for a long while, his face wet with tears, as the moon slowly climbed into the sky.

8
The Young Chief

O n the other side of the ocean, the king of
England, Charles II, leaned over a table
with members of his Privy Council, his
closest advisers. The men squinted at a
map spread out on the table, a map of the New
England colonies.

The king's advisers had been hearing a lot of
complaints lately about the way business was being
conducted by the leaders of the New England
colonies. Most of the colonists were Puritans and
other religious rebels who had left England to seek
new religious freedom. The king had given them
permission to set up colonies in his name. But people
in England claimed the colonists sought more than
religious freedom in the New World. Some said
they were trying to build empires for themselves,

by taking more and more land from the Indians. It was said the Indians, as well as many Englishmen, were not being treated fairly by the leaders of Massachusetts, Connecticut, and Plymouth, which together called themselves the United Colonies.

The king, dressed in a regal ruffled gown, rubbed his swarthy chin as his advisers reported about events in his colonies. The king had a strong dislike for Puritans and religious rebels. Such men in England had been partly responsible for chopping off the head of the king's father, Charles I. The king had a good mind to send his navy across the sea and rid his colonies of those fanatics once and for all. He thought it had been stupid to allow them to go off and start their own colonies in the first place. Now they had forgotten who was in charge over there: the king of England!

The king had so many problems at the moment—a war with the Dutch for one—that he had little time to think of his colonies. But now he was preparing to send a fleet to conquer the Dutch colony in the New World, called New Netherlands, which bordered his own colonies on the west. He could easily send someone along with the fleet to investigate matters in New England.

"Send a commissioner in my name to visit the leaders of the colonies," said King Charles II, walking away from the table.

The king wanted to make it clear that all English subjects, not just Puritans, were to be treated fairly in the colonies. He also wanted to make it clear that the colonies were to take no land from the Indians that was not freely given, and when the Indians did give up land, they gave it to the king. It was the king, then, who gave it to the colonies.

The Privy counselors saw that the king wished the meeting

45

to end. They wheeled and gave the royal salute. Then, one of them boldly looked the king in the eye and said, "Your Majesty, we shall see to it your royal command is heard, even across the vast depths of the sea."

* * *

Metacom sat by the fire in his wigwam. The first light of morning had just broken over the bay and the birds were twittering. Usually, Metacom felt peaceful at this early hour. But that morning his stomach was tight with worry. Soon he would be taken to the top of the highest hill and proclaimed chief of the Wampanoags.

His wife still lay sleeping peacefully in the dark wigwam. Metacom looked at her face, so free of worry. How he wished he could be so. He had never known how carefree he had been before Wamsutta's death. It was as if he, too, had been asleep, a sleep from which he was now rudely awakened.

It was true, he had faced his challenges, as all Wampanoag men must face theirs. He had had his skin scraped with the bone of a wolf, to make himself bleed, to purify his body, to become a man and a hunter. He had spent nights alone in the dark wilderness, without food, without sleep. He had spent days tracking wild game and learning the secrets of the forest.

When Metacom had done those things, it had seemed challenging enough. He had been learning how to survive on his own, how to catch food with his knife, his bow, and his gun; how to skin a beast and separate the meat from the furry hide; how to prepare the meat against spoilage. All these things a man must know if he is to live. But Metacom now saw that learning them was as nothing compared to what he must learn now.

Before he was merely learning to take care of himself. Now he must learn to take care of others.

Metacom stood and looked out at the quiet wigwams in the village, where his people lay sleeping. He was twenty-four years old and he looked no different than other Indian men his age. His skin was dark from being much in the sun. His body was lean and strong from hiking miles and miles each day on the forest trails, tracking and killing wild beasts, carrying their heavy carcasses on his broad back.

He had once felt he could do anything. But as he painted his face with black streaks for the ceremony, he wondered if he was suited to be a chief. Wamsutta had been taught to be a chief since he was a papoose. He had studied at the elbow of Massasoit. Now both men were gone, and there was no one to teach Metacom. He must learn to be a chief by himself, and he had to learn quickly.

There were many problems to be faced. By far the most pressing was, what should be done about the Englishmen? Many Wampanoags were convinced that Wamsutta was poisoned by the men from Plymouth. If this was true, then Metacom must act, to avenge his family and his people. Even if it was not true, the colonists had to be made to understand that a Wampanoag sachem is not one of their little children, who must come when he is summoned. But what could Metacom do to the English? They were far more powerful than his tribe was. The English had many more men and guns. Besides, the Wampanoags' friendship with the English had kept other tribes from attacking Montaup. Could Metacom afford to anger his strong allies, even if they were guilty of Wamsutta's murder?

These questions haunted Metacom that morning. He could not go to another person to ask for the answer, as a child goes

to ask a teacher's help with a difficult problem. Metacom would now be chief, which meant he had to discover all the answers himself. He sat by the fire and buried his head in his hands. How would Massasoit have reacted? Metacom could not help but wonder.

Later in the morning, when the sun was high and the day was bright and hot, Wampanoags from all over the bay area gathered at the highest point of Montaup. Hundreds of men, women, and children were seated in a circle. In the center the medicine man chanted a simple, somber hymn while dancers in broken-nosed masks shook gourd rattles and danced, kicking their legs out to their sides. This was all done to placate the evil spirits, so they would not interfere on this solemn day.

The Sakonnets were on hand with their chief, Awashonks, a husky woman with dark hair and piercing brown eyes. Awashonks had been an ally of Massasoit and Wamsutta, and was now prepared to place her tribe under the protection of the new chief. But she was watchful of young Metacom, curious to see how he would handle the duties that had suddenly fallen to him.

Weetamo and her people, the Pocassets, were there too. Weetamo's heart was still heavy with sadness over the sudden death of her husband. She would be loyal to Metacom, though she felt he had a good deal of growing up yet to do.

When the dancing was over, the medicine man stepped to the center of the hushed circle of people. He summoned Metacom to his side. The young man walked with slow, proud steps, ignoring the stares of his people. He stood before them, his bare shoulders bathed in the strong morning sun.

The medicine man looked up at the sky and chanted in a loud voice. Then he took the belt, sewn with designs in purple and white wampum shells, and slung it across Metacom's shoulder. The power was now his.

Metacom was now chief. His word would be law for all Wampanoags. He would lead them in peace, and, if need be, in war. Though the belt on his shoulders was light, the duties it stood for were heavy. Would he shrink under the weight of them? Metacom stood straight and proud. For now the people cheered him. But the questions that troubled the young chief echoed in their thoughts.

ꙶꙶꙶꙶꙶ **9** ꙶꙶꙶꙶꙶ

The Praying
Indians

The tall, slender preacher stood in the meadow, holding an open Bible. A crowd sat on the grass before him.

"The Lord told Noah, 'You must build me an ark of gopher wood,'" the preacher said, trying to make his voice deep and godlike. "'Into the ark, bring two of every kind of beast . . .'"

Some of the people on the grass giggled. The preacher ignored them and went on reading.

"'. . . two of every bird of the air, and every kind of food.'"

The people now laughed out loud. The preacher lowered his book, scowling. Then a man said, "Two of every beast and bird, they would make a big mess on the boat . . ."

The man's cheeks ballooned as he tried to smother his laughter. ". . . I think the boat would smell very bad," the man finished, bursting out laughing.

Everyone now began laughing too, which only made the preacher frown. "Very well," he said, "that will be enough of that." The preacher wiped his brow and sighed in frustration. He was not often laughed at. But now he was preaching to Indians, a tough audience.

The preacher's name was John Eliot. He had a good reason to feel frustrated. Eliot spoke to the Indians that day in their own language. He read the Bible to them, translating it into their speech as he went. It had taken Eliot years to learn the language. It was not written down in any books, since Indians had no alphabet.

Eliot was a colonial hero. Ever since Englishmen arrived in America, they talked of a "mission" to convert Indians to the Christian religion. But they could do little about it without first being able to communicate with Indians about the complex teachings of their faith. When Eliot learned the language of some Massachusetts Indians, colonists finally had someone to deliver the gospel of Christ in a voice Indians could understand.

But Eliot's first visits to preach to Indians were disappointing. The Indians just didn't take him seriously. They laughed and joked as Eliot explained the sacred faith of the English. Something new had to be tried.

In 1646 the leaders of Massachusetts, in order to get on with their pledge to "Come over and help . . ." the Indians, set up several townships for the conversion of Indians to Christianity. Eliot hoped to solve some of his missionary problems in these towns. They were to be like English settlements. Indians who lived in them had to build English-style homes, with wood floors, wood roofs, brick fireplaces and

51

Sayville Library

First missionary among the Indians

chimneys, instead of fires built on dirt floors and smoke pouring through a hole in the roof. The Indians had to wear their hair short, as Eliot believed all Christians should, and were given English clothing.

Many Indians were happy to get English clothes, but tended to wear them more casually, unbuttoned, with shirtails flapping. They could even put up with the new houses, but still slept on the floor, not on mattresses like the English.

Many of these "praying Indians" as they came to be called, didn't even mind learning about the English God and accepting him, in a way. They had grown up learning there are many spirits, or "gods," in nature. If the English wanted to teach them of one more, they couldn't see any harm in that.

On the surface, the praying Indians seemed to grow more and more like the colonists. But underneath, the soul of the Indian lived on. For example, many Indian men had more than one wife. When Indians moved to praying towns, the Puritans insisted only one wife be kept. Indian men balked. Even their wives did not want to see the other wives sent away. Often Indian men married all the sisters in a family, and the sisters were close.

Praying Indians were also loath to give up their *powwows*, or medicine men, on whom they had depended for spiritual guidance all their lives. Puritans preached to Indians about the "jealous" Christian God, who said, "Thou shalt have no other gods before Me." But praying Indians still went to ceremonies where their medicine men chanted to spirits, both good and evil.

The Puritans decided to get tough on their praying Indians. Massachusetts passed a law forbidding the worship of "false" gods. Indians could then be fined five pounds for "devil worship" with their medicine men.

The colony also passed laws to force Indians to observe the Christian sabbath. It was now against the law for Indians to fish, hunt, or even chop and carry wood on Sunday, the sabbath day, the Lord's day of rest. Indians chafed at this law too. They thought it downright silly not to be able to gather food on a Sunday, especially if they needed some. What sort of god, they wondered, would have them starve in order to "rest."

When colonists learned that adult Indians, already set in their ways, were difficult to convert to Christianity, they turned to the children. Colonists thought by catching Indians young and training them in the ways of civilization, they would have more luck. Indian children were taken from forest villages, brought to boarding schools, and taught alongside the children of white men. The Puritans had high hopes for the schooling of Indian children; however, it didn't work out very well.

Sadly, many of the Indian children, torn from their native surroundings at a young age, actually died from overexposure to English society. Wearing English clothes (instead of none), sitting in hard wooden chairs, eating English food, and catching English diseases was often too much for them. If an Indian child in a white schoolhouse didn't catch smallpox or some other deadly illness and die, he or she generally ran away or quit. However, a few Indians survived the traumas of white men's schools and even went on to college. The Puritans turned them into preachers and paraded them like show dogs.

One of these Indians was John Sassamon, a young man who lived up to Eliot's high ideal of a praying Indian. He was twenty-five years old, slender and strong of build, with close cropped black hair. He always wore a jacket and high collar, trousers, stockings and shoes, like the colonists. He spoke, read, and wrote English flawlessly. Yet, since he was a native, he could preach to Indian audiences in their own language, without Eliot's accent, which the Indians found almost as funny as his sermons.

Though Eliot's Massachusetts missions had their problems, the leaders of Plymouth Colony might have been a bit jealous of them. Massachusetts Puritans took their Christian missions very seriously. They even created Harvard College, in 1636, to train new ministers and missionaries. But Plymouth had done very little in the way of converting Indians.

It got embarrassing for Plymouth when the king's commissioner, dressed in his London finery, dropped by the governor's office one day. The commissioner asked, with one arched eyebrow, "Tell me, how are your missionaries doing with the Indians?" The governor could only blush and stammer, "Oh, very well, God be praised." But he had little actual news to report. He had no missionaries. There had been a couple on Martha's Vineyard once, but no thanks to Plymouth Colony.

It was probably just as well, because most Wampanoags— like most Indians—weren't interested in white men's religion.

Their reasons were best stated by an Iroquois Indian who once told an English minister: "We are Indians and don't wish to be turned into white men . . . As little as we desire the preacher to become Indian, so little ought he to desire the Indians to become preachers."

When Old Massasoit was alive, he had always been friendly to Eliot and the few other missionaries who came his way. He had even allowed Eliot to come to Montaup to teach Wamsutta and Metacom some English. But as far as religion was concerned, Massasoit's people had been pleased with their own.

The Wampanoags believed in a good spirit who created all things. They did not believe their god had to be the only god, as the English did. They believed, as Roger Williams wrote of other Indians, that the "Englishman's god made English men . . . but Indian gods made Indians."

The Wampanoags believed in a god they called Kiehtan, to whom all souls traveled after death. Kiehtan was said to live in a paradise "in the Southwest." Indian legends said Kiehtan was a kind and generous god who gave Indians many blessings, such as the corn and other crops they grew and ate. There was also an evil spirit, called Hobbomuck, who cursed the Indians with accidents and bad luck unless he was appeased with prayers.

Indian medicine men knew the secrets of communicating with good and evil spirits. They were respected and loved by Indians, and were a part of almost every activity, from game playing to war making.

The Wampanoags believed spirits also lived in animals and plants and in many natural events. They believed gods dwelled in the sparks made by flint stones, in the fires that warmed their wigwams, in the beating pulse of a man's blood, in his heartbeat, the breath in his lungs, and other things still deemed miraculous by modern medicine. Since the Wampanoags believed gods live in all things, even the earth and rocks, they greatly resisted giving up their land. Moreover, the earth was sacred in their eyes, because it held not only the great spirits of the rocks and trees, lakes and streams, but also the bones of the Wampanoags' ancestors, who lay buried there.

Puritans and Pilgrims thought their religious practices to be very different from the "savage" customs of the Indians. But how different were they? Indians believed rain gods brought rain for crops. During droughts, Indians prayed for rain with rain dances. Colonists called this custom "pagan." But when droughts dried and cracked their soil, they weren't above praying to their God for rain.

As for communing with good and evil spirits, colonial preachers prayed to God, their good spirit, every day. They also dealt with Satan, an evil spirit, in exorcism ceremonies. In these and other ways, colonists and Indians had similar ideas about their gods.

Soon after the king's man left Plymouth, the governor invited John Eliot in for a talk. He wanted the preacher to visit Montaup, to attempt to convert the Wampanoags. Plymouth was embarrassed by not being able to report any mission successes to the king's envoy. The governor also hoped to get a report on Metacom, who had been strangely quiet since he became chief.

Since Eliot had been a friend of Massasoit and knew many Wampanoags, he saw no harm in paying them a visit. The next afternoon he rode into Montaup, where Metacom greeted him warmly.

The last time Eliot had seen Metacom, the chief was still a carefree teenager. Eliot was impressed with the change in him now. Metacom was only twenty-five, but there was a calm air of command in his manner, in the way his people responded to him. He was their chief; there was no question of that. Eliot saw something else in Metacom's deep brown eyes, something cold and calculating, just below the surface, which had not been there when he was a teenager.

Metacom was glad to see the missionary, but he had no interest in preachers for himself or his people. "We have our own spirits of old, we do not want the Jesus lessons," the young chief said, politely but firmly.

Eliot stayed the afternoon. As he parted, he offered to send Metacom an educated Indian to improve his English. "Yes, that is good," Metacom said, grasping Eliot's hand. "Tell him to bring talking leaves." Indians called books "talking leaves," as Eliot understood very well.

The Plymouth authorities were glad Eliot was sending a language teacher to the Wampanoags. His name was John Sassamon, the Indian preacher. Now there would be at least one pair of eyes friendly to the colonists in Metacom's inner circle.

When Sassamon arrived at Montaup, Metacom put the preacher to work right away drafting a letter to the governor of Plymouth Colony. Metacom sought permission to buy a horse from Plymouth. It was illegal, at that time, for Indians to buy alcohol, guns, or horses. But special permission could be granted by the governor. The governor sent a quick reply granting Metacom's request.

Metacom went straight to Sassamon's wigwam and clapped the shy preacher heartily on the back to congratulate him. It was good to have a scribe, Metacom thought. Metacom's people were also impressed with their young chief. Not only had he refused to allow the white missionaries to come to them, but he had obtained a good educated Indian to do his writing. That wasn't bad diplomacy at all.

Metacom set off for Plymouth the following day with forty men to pick up his horse. It was the first time he had visited Plymouth since the death of Wamsutta, and the authorities were still very curious about the young chief.

The authorities greeted Metacom at the meeting house steps. The young chief surprised them. He was very cordial and polite. But they, too, noticed something in his eyes, something steely and defiant, which made them feel uncomfortable.

Metacom's horse was tied up and waiting for him in front of the meeting house. It was a doddering old cavalry horse, fit only for slow Sunday strolls. Metacom ignored the insult. He brushed the horse's mane and patted its nose lovingly. Then he mounted and rode slowly off, his band of men marching behind.

Some colonists gathered by the meeting house thought the sight of the Wampanoag chief riding off on a broken down old horse quite funny. They remembered the English name given to Metacom. It made the joke even better.

"There rides mighty King Philip on his noble steed," the men said, doubling up with laughter. They thought the young chief couldn't hear them, but he had.

Metacom bristled when the colonists laughed at him, but he didn't look back. "Yes, 'King Philip,'" he said to himself. "One day, the name will not make you laugh, it will make you weep."

10
What If Things Were as Before?

The people stood in a circle in the forest. The trees cast long shadows in the late afternoon. Metacom came forward, wearing the wampum sash of power across his chest. A man handed him a smooth club with a thick knobby tip. The crowd went silent. Metacom waved his hand to signal the guards to release the prisoner, who fell to his knees before the young chief.

Metacom swung the club over his head and drove its hardwood knob down into the man's skull. The crowd grimaced at the smack of wood on bone as the man collapsed in the dry leaves—dead.

The people watched their young chief stride silently away. It was a strange comfort to them to see him do this wicked business—the execution of a murderer—so cleanly and easily.

The people thought Metacom a good chief. When the old, the sick, and the needy came to him for food or clothing, he always had something in his wigwam, a basket of grain or a hide to keep warm in. Whenever he came upon the people, even the tiniest child, he gave of himself with a kind word, a joke, or a smile.

Still the people had their doubts about their young sachem. These doubts seemed to center around one question, "What would he do about the colonists?"

Before Wamsutta died, the Indians had come to resent the colonists more and more, for taking land, for treating them unfairly, like strangers in their own country. But the Indians had never known when to act, when to say, "You have gone far enough."

When Wamsutta died, many Wampanoags felt that the time had come to say, "This far, no farther" to the colonists, to avenge the death of Wamsutta and their pride.

Metacom spent his first few months as chief listening to a good deal of advice. Some pressed for a tougher stance against the colonists; others wished to keep the peace. Those in favor of peace were often the elderly people of the tribe, who remembered when the mighty white men had first come with their tall ships and their guns. At that time, wherever the white men went, the Indians began dying of plagues. It seemed to the Indians that the very touch of the white men was awesome and powerful. The older Indians often used the word *manittoo*, meaning, "It is a god," to describe white men and their miraculous powers. These Indians wanted peace with the white men to gain the benefit of their godliness. They also felt conflict with white men must be avoided for another reason: It is difficult to fight against gods.

But the younger Wampanoags were not so much in awe of the white men and their "magic" things. For instance, whereas the old men saw white men's guns as magic "fire sticks," young Indians owned guns and used them as the tools of their hunting trade. Though it was illegal to sell guns to an Indian, there were many English, as well as French and Dutch, who were willing to do it. To the young Wampanoags, a gun was as commonplace and necessary as a bow and arrow had been to their fathers. The magic had gone out of them.

The same was true of the colonists themselves. When these pale-faced men had first come, the Indians marveled at their light skin and delicate clothing, their shirts and trousers and petticoats and gowns, even their perfumes and powders.

These things, too, lost their charm over time. The wool that white men wore chafed Indians' skin, which they were used to leaving mostly bare. Englishmen's clothes were very uncomfortable to some Indians, with shirt collars buttoned tightly at the neck, trousers buckled snugly around the waist, and hard, high-topped leather shoes molded around the feet and ankles. Such clothes were suffocating to people accustomed to wearing simple animal skins draped loosely and comfortably. It is true that Indians coveted white people's fashions, but they wore them in their own way, unbuttoned, loosely fitting, often without shoes and belts. As for the sweet-smelling powders and perfumes of the English, their odors made Indians nauseous.

No, the young Indians were not awed anymore by white men. Metacom, perhaps more than anyone, wanted the English to pay for Wamsutta's death. But Metacom remembered Massasoit's warning to young Wamsutta: "Above all, you must protect your people. Their safety is in your hands."

This memory made Metacom question himself. His heart told him, "Take action against the English now, while you still can." But his brain told him, "You must keep them as your friends and strong allies."

61

One evening Metacom sat before the fire with a few of his friends. The men had eaten a big dinner of roast raccoon and cornmash, and they sat swigging English whiskey from a jug. Just as it was illegal to sell guns to the Indians, whiskey too was contraband—and just as easy for Indians to buy.

After the whiskey had loosened their tongues, the men began to talk loudly, about many things. When the subject turned to the colonists—as it always did—someone said, idly, "Ah, if it could only be as it was before the white men came across the great water."

That comment was enough to let loose a flood of bad feeling for the colonists in all of them. As the firelight danced in their faces, the men spoke of how they might remake their world as it was before the white men came.

"We could steal their snuff boxes," one said with a twinkle in his eye. "Then they would have to sail in a lather to England, to get more powder to shove up their noses." The men got a good belly laugh at this. As the rest got into the act, the jokes got nastier.

"We could steal their horses," said one.

"Or burn their crops," said another.

"Or shoot all their pigs and cows," said a third.

The men talked and laughed and swilled whiskey. The more whiskey they swallowed, the louder and rougher they talked.

Most of the Indians who walked past Metacom's wigwam that night probably smiled when they heard what the chief and his braves were talking about. They were frustrated, too, by pressure from the white men, and it was nice to hear someone letting off steam.

One Indian who had no steam to let off was in the wigwam next to Metacom's. John Sassamon, the Indian preacher, sat reading a book by the light of the fire. Sassamon didn't like these smoky, drafty hovels in which the Indians lived. He preferred the warm, dry English houses, like the ones his praying Indians lived in. He also didn't like being around Indians, though they were his own people, when they had been drinking. All the hooting and hollering next door in Metacom's wigwam was making him quite edgy. And they were talking so loudly that he couldn't help looking up from his book to listen.

Metacom had been quietly listening to the fun himself. He smiled as his men fought their make-believe battles. But he didn't say much, until the discussion turned to strategy.

"We could beat the English and drive them away forever, if we attack first and surprise them," one man said, leaping to his feet.

Metacom lifted his open hand and calmly said, "No, we could never defeat the English alone. There are too many of them. Our people would be crushed."

The sober, matter-of-fact way Metacom said this stunned his friends into silence. Their glorious, whiskey-fed dreams seemed to go up in the fire's smoke.

One of the younger men then seemed to pout a little. He leaned over and began scribbling like a nervous child in the dirt floor, saying, "What you say is true, sachem; we shall never be free."

These words pierced Metacom's heart. He looked at his men and spoke to them in a steady, confident voice. "We could win our freedom, someday. There is a way. But it is a way of much waiting, like waiting for the seed to sprout into stalks of ripe corn."

Metacom had everyone's attention now.

"What is the way?" someone asked.

Metacom picked up a sharp stick. He began to draw a map

of the bay area in the dirt. Then he told them his thoughts.

"We could never defeat the English alone," he said, "because they have men fanned out in many areas." He pointed to the English settlements that spread to towns all along the coast and inland almost as far as Montaup itself. "We are cornered here, in these lands and these small islands," he said, pointing to the Wampanoag lands in and around Montaup, and the Sakonnets' and Pocassets' lands to the south and east. "It would be easy for them to surround us, our homes and fields."

The men nodded and looked at Metacom differently than they had ever done before. They now understood he had done some deep thinking about the problem that weighed so heavily on them all. They listened with more respect now.

"The English have more men and better position," Metacom said. "But if we had allies to help us, we could hope to have victory," he concluded.

"Allies," one of the men said. "The English are our allies. Would new allies be like these, and become our problems?"

"It is possible," said Metacom. "But we would have no choice. We could not fight alone. It would be a fight that is over before it is begun."

The men nodded.

"We are not the only ones who hate the English," Metacom said. The word "hate" slipped past his lips before Metacom knew he had said it. But once it did, the reality of what they were doing began to strike home.

The men knew who Metacom meant. The French in Canada and the Dutch, who had scattered after their war with England, were always fighting the British, and they were well armed. They might join the Wampanoags in a war against the English colonists.

But for some reason, the men did not want to push their talk any further. They had begun by having some fun, letting off some steam. Suddenly the talk had run away with them, and they weren't sure they wanted to follow it.

"French and Dutch muskets are not good," one of them said, hoping to close off the discussion. The others agreed and the talk quickly turned to other things as the men grew sleepy with drink.

Soon the braves said goodnight and went home to sleep. As Metacom tamped out his fire that night and lay down in the dark wigwam, he felt confused. He wasn't sure if he and his men, their tongues loosened with whiskey, had merely been having a heady discussion, or if it had been something more. Had they been plotting war?

Metacom lay with his eyes wide open, staring into the dark, lost in thought. Of course a war with the Englishmen was impossible. The Wampanoags had been at peace for so very long. Their men were hunters, yes, but not warriors. There was a big difference.

Metacom tossed on his bed and sighed. One thing was true, he thought. His people were well armed. Almost all his men had rifles and they knew where to get more. Then he remembered Wamsutta and felt his old anger boil up again. Many of his people shared his wrath. Such feelings just might turn hunters into warriors, he said to himself.

However, there were always the numbers. Feelings could not change them, Metacom realized, and sighed.

During the years when the Wampanoags suffered plagues and died by the score, it had been unthinkable for them to attack the English; their numbers were just too few. Although there had been no plagues for many years and the Wampanoags' numbers had begun to grow again, the Plymouth colonists still outnumbered them by at least two to one. "The people would be crushed," Metacom concluded.

The young chief tried to clear his mind and relax, but he tossed for a long time before he could sleep. By the following morning, though, Metacom had forgotten all about the previous night's party and wild speculation about war. It was as if it had never happened.

A few days later, Metacom was shocked when a messenger rode into Montaup with a summons for him to appear before the Plymouth General Court. Metacom was livid. "Again, the colonists feel they can order a sachem to do something," Metacom thought. It was maddening. They may "invite," they may "suggest," but the colonists could not "order" him, Metacom fumed. Orders were given to slaves.

Metacom decided to go to Plymouth anyway. But he would not go sniveling and whimpering, licking their boots. He would go as a sachem or, in the words of the English, a king—King Philip.

The next day, Metacom marched into Plymouth, flanked by eighty armed men. There were the usual chuckles from the prim Plymouth passers-by when they saw the Indians in their rag-tag casual style of dress. But the laughter was quieted by the steely stares of Metacom and his men. They were in no mood for nonsense.

When Metacom greeted the Plymouth officials, he was aloof and formal. The officials noticed his coolness and wasted no time with false pleasantries. They had been told the Wampanoag chief was planning to join the Dutch and the French in making war on Plymouth and the English colonies. They wanted an explanation.

Metacom felt a tug in his chest. "How could they know," he thought.

The guilty look on Metacom's face was all the Plymouth authorities needed to convict him in their hearts. But they still went through the formalities.

"We command that you appear before our General Court on June 1, year of our Lord 1667, to answer these charges."

Metacom collected himself. He had not actually plotted to attack anyone. He had merely been drinking and talking—perhaps talking too much—but just talking. A sachem has the right to talk to his own people, he thought, without apologizing to anyone for what he says.

"I will answer the charges now," Metacom said sharply. "I have planned nothing against your colony," he raged, and quite truthfully. He had talked, even speculated, but he had not planned any attack. Indeed, he had decided that to do so would be foolish.

The authorities eyed Metacom suspiciously. They obviously did not believe him.

Metacom, seeing their doubts, wished to allay them. "A

break with the English would be little less painful than death to me," he said, with false emotion. "It would be a source of joy to my enemies and grief to my friends."

The authorities were mollified, but still unconvinced. "Nevertheless," one said, stepping up to the sachem. "You and your men will leave your guns here until this matter is cleared up."

Metacom's face went red with rage, but what was he to do? If he refused, it would only convince the authorities he was guilty and give them an excuse to attack his people. All Indians still remembered what happened to the Pequots when they unwittingly gave the white men such an excuse. He would do as they asked.

A small crowd of colonists watched as the Wampanoags walked quietly to the courthouse steps and laid their rifles in a pile. Metacom could sense their shame. Only a few hours before, they had strode into town with haughty pride. Now they struck the trail back to Montaup, stripped of their weapons, and not a little of their pride.

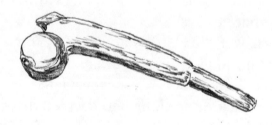

11

Puppet on a String

Word of the Wampanoags' supposed plotting spread fast in Plymouth. Soon the townspeople were talking about how arrogantly "King Philip" had acted and how full of "sinful" pride he was. The Plymouth colonists had taken to calling Metacom "King Philip" now, as a sarcastic joke. They actually thought him no better than a savage child of Satan, the furthest thing from royalty.

It was easy for the people in Plymouth to believe Metacom was plotting to attack them. After Wamsutta had been treated so poorly, it would have been remarkable if the Wampanoags didn't at least think about getting revenge. Though it was only human for the Wampanoags to think about revenge, the people of Plymouth were downright furious about it.

The Pilgrims had been convinced since the day they first set foot on Plymouth soil that the New World was destined to be theirs, a gift from God. They even thanked God for sending plagues to clear the Indians away.

Now, after living in Plymouth for fifty long years, the Pilgrims were more convinced than ever that the land in this country was their gift from the creator. If the treacherous King Philip would even think of making war on them, it was further proof that he and his people were children of the devil. Only Satan's offspring would plot against the children of God.

If the colonists ever felt guilty about driving the Indians off their land, if the sight of Indian women and children being pushed into the wilderness with their belongings strapped on their backs ever made the colonists feel ashamed, they had a ready salve to spread on their aching souls. After all, they would say, the Indians weren't using the land anyway. They merely "roamed" over it. Englishmen would "improve" the land by cutting down trees, building farmhouses, fencing in cattle, and clearing fields for planting. In other words, the colonists would make good use of land that would otherwise go to waste—or so they thought.

On the other hand the Indians didn't understand the colonists. Not only did the Indians use the land, but they loved it just the way it was, and didn't think it needed any "improving." Indians hunted wild game and wanted to keep the woodlands wild so that the game would stay there. To Indians, cutting down trees and scaring away the animals in the forest was not "improving" the land at all.

Indians also couldn't understand why the English penned in cattle and hogs. If they had only left the forests alone, there

would have been plenty of wild animals for everyone. There would have been no need for fenced hog yards or cow pastures; no need to bother with feeding and watering the animals, either, for wild animals take care of themselves.

At Montaup, Metacom thought about his day in court. The colonists had caught him off guard with their accusation. But he was innocent after all. He hadn't plotted anything. He and his men had merely had a spirited discussion. And what of it? Surely a chief is permitted to discuss what he wants with his friends. Metacom grew more indignant the more he thought about the English charges against him.

Metacom pieced together what had happened. One of his people—he had no idea whom—had spread word that he intended to make an alliance with the Dutch and French against Plymouth, even though he had only hinted at the possibility.

Metacom wished he could get his hands on the man who had betrayed him.

Metacom walked into Sassamon's wigwam. The preacher was bent over a small desk, reading and taking notes with a quill pen. Metacom put his hand on Sassamon's shoulder. "I have been betrayed," he said gravely.

Sassamon's eyes grew wide. He seemed uneasy. He cleared his throat and quickly asked, "Who has done this, my sachem?"

"I do not know. But I must find him out. A cloud of suspicion hangs over our people," Metacom said.

Metacom explained to the preacher what happened in court. Sassamon seemed relieved. He breathed a deep sigh and said, "One of your own men may have a loose tongue, but a Wampanoag would never bring secrets to the ears of the Plymouth men."

Metacom nodded. "Yes, you are right. But who?"

Sassamon rubbed his chin and pondered. "If one of our men made foolish boasts, to a Narragansett, let us say, then the riddle is solved. For a Narragansett would give your words the darkest cast, and deliver them to the English for a glass of whiskey."

Metacom paced back and forth quietly for a while. "Yes," he said finally, "that is what happened. A Narragansett heard of our talk and went to Plymouth to tell them we are plotting war, though our talk was the talk of drunken men."

The next day, Metacom went back to Plymouth. He demanded to know the identity of the Indian who had brought the story of his plot. The authorities agreed to tell. The informer was a Narragansett, they said, a man whom Metacom knew to be a drunk and a liar. Sassamon had been right. Metacom did not pause to wonder how his aide had guessed the truth. He was too angry for that.

"You would not take the word of an Indian sachem in your court against an English criminal, but you will take the word of an Indian scoundrel against that of a sachem," Metacom scoffed. "And this you call justice."

It was true. The colonists didn't accept Indian statements against white men in court. In this case, however, they were content to accept the word of an Indian scamp against that of a chief.

Roger Williams wrote a letter to the Plymouth authorities backing up Metacom's charge that his Narragansett accuser was a "vile fellow." After Williams's letter arrived, the authorities softened. They returned the Wampanoags' guns, though they charged Metacom forty pounds for court costs.

Metacom and his men silently picked up their rifles from the stack on the courthouse steps. Plymouth citizens lined both sides of the street and watched from windows as the Wampanoags filed by. Metacom was saddened that his people had to be humiliated this way, herded like common criminals, like slaves.

It had been this way since Massasoit died. First the colonists had "summoned" Wamsutta with a gun poked in his ribs—to his death. Now Metacom was seized, harrassed, and punished for remarks he made to friends in his own wigwam. Metacom and his people were being controlled like puppets, and Plymouth held all the strings.

There were uneasy relations for the next few years between Montaup and Plymouth. Many a time Metacom was called to the courthouse to respond to some charge or other. The young chief was always proud and defiant.

Metacom still wished to keep the peace, but he was not prepared to make slaves of his people to do it. He and his people began to collect guns and make bows and arrows, in case they had to defend themselves. It seemed Metacom wanted to avoid the fate of the Pequots by making sure his people were ready for anything.

One day Sassamon questioned Metacom about the people's growing concern with collecting weapons and even training themselves in the tactics of war. Metacom explained his fears to his scribe, whom he had grown closer to over the years. Then Sassamon had an idea. "You are preparing for war, should you not also prepare for the consequences of war," Sassamon said.

Sassamon advised Metacom to prepare a last will and testament, in case he were killed in a skirmish with the colonists. "If they kill you, they will say your land belongs to them. You must prepare a piece of paper, bequeathing your land to your kin and your people."

Metacom wasn't sure it was necessary, but he saw no harm in drawing up a will as the Englishmen did. Perhaps Sassamon was right, he thought. The colonists placed great faith in pieces of paper. Perhaps he should draw up a piece of paper to tell what should happen to his land and belongings if he should die. Then no court could say it belonged to the English. If a will would ensure his people against losing their land, he would have one. In any case, what harm could come of it?

Sassamon drew up a will in English. Metacom could speak the language, but could not read it very well, so Sassamon read the document to the chief. Metacom then took a quill pen and signed the will with his English name, King Philip.

12

Naughty King Philip

The English trader finished stacking the rifles outside the chief's wigwam. He mopped his sweaty brow with his bandana, brushed his whiskers, and turned to Metacom, who stood inspecting one of the rifles. "We must draw up a bill of sale for the land you are trading me for these weapons," the trader said. "But we must not mention the guns." He winked.

Metacom was well aware that the trader's life would be in danger if other colonists knew he was selling guns to Indians. "We will write that you gave me clothing," Metacom said. "No one shall know the truth."

Metacom led the trader into Sassamon's wigwam, where he knew he would find some paper and a pen to draw up a bill of sale. Sassamon was sitting by his fire, reading a book. Metacom led the trader to Sassamon's desk, where paper, a pen, and a bottle of ink were arranged neatly. Sassamon looked up from his book just as the trader was picking up from the desk the rolled parchment containing Metacom's last will and testament. Sassamon's face went pale with fright.

The trader absent-mindedly unrolled the document and said, "Well, what have we here?" Metacom shrugged, "It is nothing, a piece of paper, but my friend says it may be important some day." Metacom pointed to where Sassamon was sitting, but the preacher was gone.

"Strange," said Metacom. "Where did he go so quickly?" Metacom's question was answered when the trader read the will aloud.

"You are very generous with your praying Indian," the trader said. "It says here that, if you should die, all of your lands and property will go to John Sassamon."

Metacom was shocked. "It cannot be," he said. The trader assured him. "It's all spelled out right here: John Sassamon is to inherit all that you own."

Metacom had been tricked. His supposed friend was not a friend after all. He was a liar and a thief.

Metacom quickly dispatched men in every direction to find Sassamon. But the wily preacher had disappeared without a trace. It seemed he had planned for a quick getaway, in case his treachery was uncovered. Sassamon had tricked Metacom. The chief now believed the preacher was working for the Englishmen, and would have turned over the Wampanoags' land to the colonists in the event of his death. Metacom flew into a rage and cursed Sassamon to the four winds.

A few days later, an armed band of Plymouth men rode into Montaup. They brought Metacom another summons to appear in court. The chief, still suspicious from the Sassamon episode, sensed a trap. He refused to go unless the colonists sent one of their men to Montaup, to be held until Metacom was safely back home. The Plymouth men rode out, frustrated.

Metacom knew they would soon be back. He felt a showdown might be coming.

The people of Montaup, at the chief's command, continued to make bows and arrows and gather guns. Metacom wanted to be ready in case Plymouth was planning any surprises.

Soon the Plymouth men returned. This time they agreed to send the hostage Metacom had requested. The date for the meeting was set.

On a clear morning in April 1671, just fifty years after Massasoit had signed a treaty of friendship with Plymouth Colony, the English hostage, Richard Williams, surrendered himself to the Wampanoags. Metacom placed him under guard and led a band of one hundred armed men to the town of Taunton, northeast of Montaup, where he would meet with the leaders of Plymouth. If the colonists had it in mind to ambush him, he would be ready.

When Metacom and his men were a few miles outside Taunton, the chief stopped by a stream and sent scouts ahead. They sighted a very large band of colonial men at arms on the other side of Taunton. The colonists had more than twice as many men as the Indians, and all were armed with rifles. Some dressed in armored suits. Though many of Metacom's men had rifles as well, a lot had only bows and arrows. Metacom was outnumbered and outgunned. He would not enter Taunton like that.

Metacom sent word that he would like to negotiate. The colonists, somewhat upset, sent a representative. It was agreed that equal numbers of armed men would approach Taunton, and the rest would stay behind. Metacom went ahead cautiously with a smaller band of men.

At the church in Taunton, the Wampanoags lined up on one side, the colonists on the other. There they faced each other down while Metacom went inside to talk with the leaders of Plymouth and some other Massachusetts Bay leaders who had also decided to attend.

As soon as the meeting began, Metacom realized he had made a mistake by coming. The Plymouth authorities accused him of preparing to make war on the colonists. Metacom wanted to say he was preparing his people to defend themselves in case the English attacked; however, they would not believe this. He lied: "We prepare to make war on the Narragansetts," he said. But he was a poor liar, and the attempt only made the colonists more furious.

"You are seeking to make war, without cause, on the colonists," one of the men repeated. "There have been Narragansetts sighted in your camp. You do not seek to make war on them, but to ally with them, against us. Can you deny this?"

Metacom didn't know what to say. He gazed through the door, at the armed colonists outside. If he denied these charges, he felt the colonists would fall on his own ill-trained troops. His men would not stand a chance against them. He decided to pretend to agree to whatever these men said, and get his men out of this trap. Then when he and his men were free, they would indeed prepare for war against the English, since that seemed to be what the English wanted.

Metacom confessed to all the charges, and he signed a new "treaty" the colonists drew up. It was a humiliating document that put him and his people under the rule of Plymouth Colony, as well as the king, in all matters from then on. It also said Metacom, through the "naughtiness" of his heart, had broken the treaty made by his father with the colonists. Metacom would have signed anything to get his men safely away that day. There would be another day, he thought, when marks on papers would be forgotten.

The "treaty" said that Metacom would surrender all the weapons held by his people, beginning with his men present at Taunton. The chief, wishing to appear compliant, ordered his men to pile their rifles on the steps of the church. Some of the men were openly angry with Metacom. Their rifles were their most prized possessions. But all agreed to leave them, perhaps realizing they were in an impossible situation.

Humiliated, Metacom and his men went back to Montaup. On the long walk, angry words were muttered against the young chief. The men thought he had sold them out.

Back at Montaup, Metacom ordered the English hostage released. Then he met with his council to discuss the day's events. The chiefs in his council were of a lower rank than Metacom, but their agreement was needed on all actions taken. They had signed today's treaty, too, on Metacom's advice. Now they wanted an explanation.

"The guns we gave up today were a small price to pay for our lives. We can get more guns, but of lives, we each have only one," the young chief answered solemnly. One of the lower chiefs was not satisfied. "Bah, you have made fools of us," he said. "I will never again serve under you. You have disgraced our people." This chief then stormed out of the council house.

There were many angry voices raised against the young chief that night at Montaup. They were outraged that Metacom had promised to surrender all the Wampanoags' guns, not just the ones his men had carried that afternoon. But Metacom never planned to comply with that part of the treaty. He had been buying time and his men's freedom by signing it. Now he would ignore it and try to win back the loyalty of his people.

First Metacom instructed his people to hide their weapons and not to give them up under any circumstances. Many of the people then began to believe that Metacom meant what he said, that he had not surrendered, only bought time to regroup.

Metacom then spread word to his people of the treachery of his former aide, John Sassamon. Someone had gone to the English and told them the Wampanoags were preparing to make war. Metacom suspected Sassamon, who had fled Montaup in disgrace. Metacom tried to lift the blame for the Wampanoags' disgrace from his own shoulders and place it on Sassamon's, where he felt it belonged.

When the Wampanoags did not surrender their guns, the English sent a group of messengers to Montaup. This gave Metacom a chance to win back his people's affection and loyalty.

A celebration was in progress when the messengers from Plymouth, James Brown and a companion, arrived at Montaup. Metacom and several of his friends had been drinking, and they were in no mood to show any respect to the English. When the dancing stopped, the messengers approached Metacom. The chief was standing by the fire, in full view of the whole town.

In the old days of Massasoit, messengers from Plymouth came humbly before the chief. They removed their hats, bowed, and kissed his hand. But Brown stood insolently before Metacom, his hat on his head, and barked, "You must appear in Plymouth Colony to explain why you have not surrendered your guns, as you promised to do."

Metacom decided it was high time the colonists showed some respect for a Wampanoag sachem again.

"You dare to come before me like this," Metacom raged. "You would not go before your King Charles with your hat on your head. Is the Wampanoag king entitled to less respect?"

Metacom lunged at the messenger and slapped the hat off his head. The people laughed when they saw their chief humiliate the colonist. Brown's blushing face only made them laugh harder. With one swipe of his hand, Metacom had again endeared himself to his people.

The next morning a sober Metacom told the messengers he could not go to Plymouth, for he had to travel to Boston first, to speak to the leaders of Massachusetts. The messengers returned to Plymouth, outraged by Metacom's defiance. Meanwhile, Metacom went to Boston, where he won the sympathy of the Massachusetts Bay Colony's leaders. They felt Plymouth had overstepped itself with the Wampanoags.

But the Massachusetts officials went back on their word to Metacom at a meeting with the colonists from Connecticut and Plymouth. Now all these men condemned Metacom and the Wampanoags. They again gave Metacom a humiliating treaty to sign, making him agree to put himself and his people under Plymouth's power. Metacom also agreed to pay one hundred pounds to Plymouth, as a tribute. But the agreement was half-hearted. He never intended to keep it. He was buying more time. And Metacom had won a victory, for the treaty made no mention of the surrender of any more guns, and the matter was forgotten.

Now that the pressure from Plymouth was temporarily off the Wampanoags, Metacom set out to plan in earnest for what he knew must come. He was not concerned with the weapons his people had already lost. New weapons could be bought. What he needed was more fighting men.

Before, Metacom had armed his people for defense, in case the Plymouth men attacked the Wampanoags the way the Pequots were once attacked. Now Metacom hardened his heart for war. The colonists continued to demand his presence at "meetings" at their pleasure. They acted as if they owned the country. In the old days they were guests. Now they behaved like lords. Metacom could not allow their insults to go unanswered.

He felt his people would go to war if he asked them to. But they could not win by themselves. There were now some 40,000 white men in New England, but only 20,000 Indians. Worse, the Indians in Metacom's tribe numbered only a couple of thousand.

Even with the help of every Indian in New England, the Wampanoags would be severely outnumbered. Only with a sound strategy, and some powerful allies, could the Indians drive the colonists out of their settlements and back across the sea. Without allies, all was lost.

13

A Violent Twisting of the Neck

On a January evening, in 1675, the governor of Plymouth Colony showed John Sassamon to his front door and shook hands with the preacher. "Thank you for the information," the governor said. "You have been most helpful."

Sassamon took up his rifle, bundled up against the cold, and walked out into the night.

No one knows what happened to Sassamon after he left the governor's house. A month later, some travelers found Sassamon lying dead under the ice at Assowomset pond in present-day Middleborough. On the surface of the ice, near the body, lay his hat and gun, and a brace of ducks, now frozen stiff, which he had apparently shot.

It looked as if Sassamon had slipped on the ice and hit his head, and the accidental blow had killed him. That's what the men who found the body told the authorities after they buried Sassamon near the pond.

There the matter stood for months. Then the authorities in Plymouth grew suspicious: perhaps Sassamon had not died by accident. They knew why Sassamon had gone to the governor's house that night—to tell him that Metacom was recruiting Indians to wage war on Plymouth. The colony now suspected foul play.

Plymouth acted quickly. The body was exhumed and an autopsy was performed. The authorities said they found blood still flowing from wounds on Sassamon's corpse. They also said no water flowed from the body, so that Sassamon couldn't have drowned. There was even mention of evidence of a "violent twisting" of the deceased man's neck. These facts, declared Plymouth, pointed to only one possible cause of death—murder.

The people of Plymouth thought some Wampanoags had murdered Sassamon, on Metacom's orders, because the preacher had been talking to Plymouth about Metacom's activities. Soon they found a witness who said he had seen three Wampanoags kill Sassamon.

But the witness was himself suspicious. He was a praying Indian, named Patuckson, who was friendly to the colonists. It was said Patuckson owed a gambling debt to one of the men he accused. The authorities didn't seem to think it mattered. They scheduled a murder trial on the strength of the lone Indian's word. In most cases, the word of an Indian would not even be considered, and in murder cases a minimum of two witnesses was usually required to convict a man. But this was no ordinary case. Plymouth apparently wanted to teach Metacom a lesson, and the colony was willing to bend its normal rules.

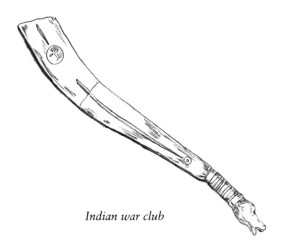

Indian war club

Metacom himself went to Plymouth to insist he had nothing to do with the death of his former assistant. The Plymouth authorities said they would let the evidence decide. They put Metacom on his "best behavior." They were used to treating Metacom as a child and didn't hesitate to do so again.

The Wampanoags were furious. Many were quick to point out that even if Metacom had ordered Sassamon's execution, he had every right, as chief, to do so. Sassamon had betrayed Metacom in the matter of the will, and he was on Wampanoag property. But Plymouth pressed ahead with the trial.

Tension mounted between the colonists and the Indians. Armed bands of Wampanoags were seen wandering about outside of English settlements; their attitude toward settlers was reported to be very hostile. What if the stories about Metacom's plotting were true, the colonists thought. Would a guilty verdict against the accused Wampanoags bring Metacom's men swarming out of Montaup to attack their towns?

As for Metacom and his plotting, he had indeed been traveling among the towns of nearby Indians trying to drum up support for his war. He hadn't met with much success, however.

The scene was generally the same. Metacom would appear before the men of the town, gathered about the council fire.

He would speak about the old life of the Indians, before the white men came, when they alone possessed the green forests and white beaches of their ancestors. Metacom told how that glorious life could be theirs again, if all Indians would join him in a war with the colonists.

Each time Metacom spoke, the young men in the crowd eyed him intently. They loved his stories of forgotten times, when Indians ruled the land. They even believed they remembered those days, though, like Metacom, they had lived near white men all their lives, and had not lived in the days when there were no white men in America.

Strangely, older Indians, some who were old enough to remember the days before white men came, generally scowled as Metacom spoke. They thought the young sachem's plan foolish. Was he mad? The English could not be beaten. Even if they could be, was it wise? The English provided them with goods and protection. Why spoil a good thing?

Metacom made little progress with his talks to other bands of Indians. Nevertheless, the two largest tribes in southeastern New England, the Narragansetts and the Nipmucks, were now wavering. They would remain neutral, although they might be persuaded to join in the fighting later, if there ever was any fighting. This was the best that Metacom had been able to get.

Other tribes were opposed to his plan. The Niantics of western Rhode Island, the Mohegans of Connecticut, and the Massachusetts tribe to the north, were convinced that white men were simply too powerful to defeat. Even the Sakonnets, part of Metacom's own people, were wavering. Their sachem, Awashonks, would give Metacom no definite answer about joining his cause.

As the trial approached, tensions mounted. Metacom knew his army was still too small to go to war. But if Plymouth were

to execute the Wampanoags for murder, Metacom might lose the luxury of waiting any longer. Young men from other tribes, moved by Metacom's speeches, were joining the Wampanoags daily at Montaup. If the Wampanoags were hanged, Metacom might not be able to control them.

All eyes were on events in the packed courtroom when the trial began. Four Indians were put on the jury, a highly unusual move. Plymouth said it sat the Indians on the panel to ensure that "justice" was done. But the Indians were not given the power to cast votes of guilt or innocence. They were there merely to advise the regular jury, made up entirely of colonists.

The trial moved quickly. The three Wampanoag defendants were Mattashunnamo, his son Wampapaquan, and a friend named Tobias. All three pleaded innocent to the charges. But their accuser, Patuckson, calmly told the court he had seen the three murder Sassamon. The jury retired to consider. After a brief caucus, they returned and found all three defendants guilty of murder. The judge sentenced them to be hanged.

As the three men, knees buckling, stood atop horses, the hangman tied blindfolds over their eyes. He took ropes dangling from branches overhead and noosed them around their necks. Someone cracked a whip, the horses ran off, the men fell, and the ropes pulled taut. The necks of Mattashunnamo and Tobias snapped immediately. They were dead in an instant. But Wampapaquan's rope broke, not his neck, and he found himself lying on the damp ground looking up at his father's lifeless body swinging back and forth in the air above him. Miraculously, Wampapaquan was saved.

Or was it a miracle? The authorities took Wampapaquan aside and again pressed him to confess to the murders. The Indian, knowing his father and friend were now beyond harm, blamed them for the murder. He also said that the two were acting on orders from Metacom. Now that Plymouth had the confession it wanted, Wampapaquan was hanged again. This time, the rope worked just fine.

Word spread quickly in Wampanoag country. Many people felt the trial was a sham. Some thought Plymouth had purposely hanged Wampapaquan with a frayed rope the first time, in the hopes he would incriminate his companions after they were dead and implicate Metacom. Now Plymouth had an excuse to further persecute the Wampanoag sachem.

The Wampanoags were outraged. Not only was the trial a sham, it was unnecessary. The killing happened on Indian land. It was an Indian matter, regardless of who had done it. The colonial courts had no business trying or executing anyone.

The scene at Montaup was tense. Metacom was livid, but he did not wish to attack yet. Many of his men accused him of cowardice. But it was not cowardice. He still wanted time to secure allies. The English were too powerful. The young men whom Metacom had inflamed with his preaching would not wait any longer, however. The English had gone too far. A band of men, painted for war, stole out of Montaup and headed up the peninsula to Swansea, the nearest white settlement.

The Indians arrived at Swansea whooping and hollering through the streets and shooting off their guns. The frightened people gathered in a few log cabins and barricaded the doors and windows. The Indians set fire to some empty farmhouses and began looting others.

At Montaup, Metacom saw the big black plumes of smoke rising from Swansea. He had waited a long time to see such a sight. He had always known that Swansea, on the gateway to his own peninsula, would be the first English town to fall when the Indians rose. But not now, he thought. Not yet!

14

"He Sent Our Enemies to Be Our Lords"

The nervous Sunday crowd in the Plymouth church hushed as the preacher mounted the pulpit. He grasped the oak rail with his slender hands and said, "Brethren, we have strayed too far from the path of almighty God."

The people nodded to one another. They knew what the preacher meant. But he spelled it out for them anyway.

"What does it mean, when the savage steals from us, burns down our homes, kills the cattle in our fields?" the preacher asked. He paused and looked skyward—to heaven—and answered his own question.

"It means He has sent our enemies to be our lords," the preacher ranted. In other words, God had sent the Indians to punish the colonists for forgetting Him.

"We have forgotten the mission that brought our fathers and mothers to these shores," the preacher continued. "That mission is a simple one: to live a pure Christian life. But how many of us do? Many no longer even come to church on Sunday."

The people cast their eyes down in shame. Each of them had missed a meeting now and then. The meeting house in Plymouth was a long way from some of their farms. Many had to spend all day Sunday just walking to meeting and back again, over miles and miles of muddy roads. It was only natural to miss some Sundays.

A "Day of Humiliation" was to be held in the colony, the preacher said. On that day, people would humble themselves before God, admit their sins, and begin living the Christian life again. Then, perhaps, God would forgive them and stop the Indian menace.

After the rioting caused by the hanging of the three Wampanoags, Swansea was quiet once more. No Indians had been sighted for hours. A group of men and a young boy found the courage to patrol the smoky streets. They quickly spotted a group of Indians sneaking out of a house, sacks filled with stolen goods slung over their shoulders. One of the men barked, "Fire on them." The little boy, who held a big rifle, aimed his weapon and fired. One of the Indians collapsed to the ground. The others carted him off.

Later the Indians came back to town to see the Englishmen. "Our friend has died," one of the Indians said gravely. The Englishmen were speechless. They didn't know whether the Indians were looking for condolences or a fight.

The little boy who shot the Indian stood by listening. "Oh, what does it matter, it was only an Indian," he said.

The Indians were indignant. In a rage, they stomped off. One of the colonists ran after them. "He's just a boy. He doesn't mean what he says," the man screamed. But the Indians did not turn back.

Up until this time the Indians had burned and looted, but had not killed. Now they raised their war hatchets.

In a village nearby, settlers walked to an abandoned barn to get sacks of corn for the people of Swansea. A group of Indians, crouching in the brush by the side of the road, leaped out whooping and screaming. The Indians shot and killed six of the settlers. One of them was the little boy who had killed the Indian the night before.

Later in the day, Indians ambushed a group of people walking along the road returning from church. One man was killed and others were wounded.

That night an Indian stole close to one of the garrison houses. The Indian shot a soldier guarding the door and fled into the night as the wounded man bled to death. Later two nervous colonists dashed from the garrison house, heading to Rehoboth for a doctor to tend the wounded churchgoers. The next morning the men's mutilated corpses were found by the roadside. Nine colonists in all were killed and two more mortally wounded on June 24, 1675.

When reports of dead colonists reached Metacom, he flew into a rage. He had wanted to wait, at least a little longer. He had sent runners to the Narragansetts and the Nipmucks. He might have gotten help in a few days. Now he had no time left. Once his men spilt the blood of Englishmen, the war had begun, whether he liked it or not.

Metacom met with Unkompoin, his uncle and war chief, and Annawon, a brave young warrior. Metacom drew a map in the dirt with a stick, and laid out the first phase of the Wampanoags' war strategy. They hoped Metacom would still be able to persuade allies to join their struggle. But for now the

Wampanoags were on their own.

Meanwhile, more volunteer soldiers arrived in Swansea. They were young, fresh-faced men from Rehoboth, Taunton, and Plymouth, under the command of Captain Cudworth, a tall, broad-shouldered man with graying hair and long experience as a soldier in England.

Once the Indians began to kill colonists, Cudworth wanted to go after them. But reports said Metacom had nearly 1,000 warriors. Cudworth's 200 soldiers might not be enough. The captain decided to wait in the garrison until more soldiers arrived from Massachusetts Bay. Meanwhile, the Indians, without an army to oppose them, raided the small settlements beyond Swansea.

By the time the Massachusetts troops arrived, four days had passed since the first colonists had been killed. The army thought Metacom and his men were trapped on the peninsula. They believed they could march in, when they were good and ready, and wipe the Indians out. They planned to end the war quickly.

Finally, on June 30, the army moved slowly out of Swansea, down the peninsula. The foot soldiers were flanked by men on horseback.

The long march down the peninsula was dismal. On both sides of the road lay the blackened rubble of homes torched by Metacom's men. A little farther on, the young soldiers' knees buckled at a gory sight. A group of wooden poles were planted upright. Rammed atop each dripped the severed head of a colonist. The young men, their faces pale with fright, buried the heads and pressed grimly toward Montaup.

When the army reached Montaup, all was quiet. The men poked their guns into the quiet wigwams and peeked inside. All were empty. The cornfields were deserted. The men pushed ahead to the southern shore. Not a soul was there. They kicked through the thick brush along the banks. Not a single canoe was found. Metacom and the Wampanoags, who were thought to be "trapped" on the peninsula, were gone.

The soldiers were far from upset that the enemy was absent. They whistled and cheered. Many believed the war was now over, since they had occupied the enemy's home base. They talked gaily about what to do with their new territory, so easily won. "This land will make us a handsome sum of silver," many said.

Benjamin Church, one of the soldiers, stood by the water's edge and peered across to the misty bogs beyond the other shore. Church, a bearded, broad-shouldered man, had spent a lot of time among Indians in the area. He didn't believe Metacom would give up so easily.

Church cast a sweeping look toward the swamps of Pocasset. As he squinted in the dusky light, he imagined he saw proud King Philip, standing in the tall marsh grass, laughing.

15

A Proper
Feast

warrior Annawon
e ankle-deep water
king on the sentries
ath to Weetamo's

Cudworth's troops
met Metacom on
er fleet of canoes.
anoags across the
over an hour, but
vas removed from
ople in the Pocasset

Now wampanoag fighting men were spread out
in small groups throughout the swamp. Well-hidden

in the branches of trees and the tall marsh grass, they kept watch day and night.

Metacom had been quick to evacuate Montaup once he received news that colonists had been killed. He didn't want to be trapped on his peninsula by the oncoming English troops.

Once the Wampanoags were safely on the other shore, Metacom put his men on alert. When his scouts reported that the Massachusetts troops had arrived at Montaup, he was sure an attack would follow swiftly. He waited, but no attack came. Metacom was puzzled. Why did they not come? Were they more fearful than he thought? Or did they think his people presented no danger?

At Montaup, the English troops decided to protect the land they had "captured" rather than go after the Wampanoags. They began building a fort of logs and stone to garrison their troops against the Wampanoags' possible return. Meanwhile, the 200 Massachusetts troops were called off on another mission, to keep the Narragansetts in line.

Church grew impatient. He felt the commanders were not taking Metacom seriously. His anger mounted. If they were here to fight Indians, he said, they should find some Indians to fight. Cudworth, at length, decided to give in to the excitable Church and allowed him to take a small band of soldiers across the inlet to the Pocasset shore.

The Wampanoag scouts saw the soldiers approaching and quickly reported back to Metacom and his war chief, Unkompoin. The plan was to lay low and draw the men deep into the swamp before firing on them. This way, they might get them all before any had a chance to escape and give away their positions.

The English split into two groups of about twenty men each. One group quickly ran against some of Metacom's men.

The impatient Indians, instead of drawing the soldiers into the trap, started shooting. The outgunned English fled to the waterfront and were rescued by their boats.

A little to the south, Church picked up footprints in the mud and led his men in pursuit of what he hoped would be their first action. Instead, they ran directly into a nest of rattlesnakes. The men froze in panic as the black serpents slithered toward them through the marshwater. Forgetting about Indians, they fled back to the shore. Church had little choice but to stop leading for the moment and follow his terrified men.

On the shore, Church's men found themselves pinned down by Indian gunfire. They took shelter behind trees, but the Indians were relentless. The English held the Indians off for hours, until darkness approached. Church knew that if he and his men didn't escape, Indians would fall on them in the night. Luckily for the sore and tired colonists, a boat got to the shore in time and they were dragged on board and brought to safety.

After that first failure at swamp warfare, the English commander decided not to risk any more such maneuvers. They would continue to build their fort and wait for Metacom's return, which they felt must come soon. Then the English would have the Indians for target practice from atop the strong stone walls of the fort, and the war would quickly be over. It was the way wars were supposed to be fought.

Metacom and his war leaders had no plans whatsoever to return to Montaup. When they saw the English building the fort, they could not understand why. The Englishmen's concept of "proper" warfare, and of the war being "over" when one's home base is lost, would have seemed strange to the Indians. To them the war went on while there were people still alive to fight it. The Englishmen soon understood.

Metacom and his men were not merely sitting and waiting for the English troops. On several occasions bands of Wampanoags stole out of the bog and into the woods around nearby English settlements. Without warning, they sprang from the woods, swinging their battle clubs, burning outlying farmhouses, killing anyone they found. They attacked the town of Taunton, killing several Englishmen and burning houses. They almost demolished Dartmouth to the south, leaving nearly every building in flames when they slipped back into the forest.

As long as the colonists refused to come into the swamp after them, the Wampanoags could use it as a base for raids. The colonists, however, weren't the Wampanoags' only enemy.

The long midsummer days languishing in the hot, muggy swamp were taking their toll on Metacom's people. Though they were accustomed to snakes and the other hazards of the swamps, life there was still very uncomfortable. For one thing, the air was thick with mosquitoes and other insects. The men found their skin covered with red sores from dozens of bug bites a day. And there was little food. Indians were experts at living off the land. They could always eat snake meat, or even toad. But it was difficult, even for these rugged woodsmen, to live on such fare for too long.

Metacom spent many hours in Weetamo's village, where the women and children were lodged, talking to his sister-in-law. With the help of Annawon and Unkompoin, he finally persuaded her and her war chiefs to fight for his cause. It had not been easy to convince Weetamo. She had been at peace as long as the rest of the Wampanoags, and her people were no more prepared for war than Metacom's. But now that fighting had started and the Wampanoags were as yet unscathed, she seemed encouraged. Perhaps there was something to Metacom's madness, Weetamo thought.

Meanwhile, English settlements as far south as Stonington and as far west as Hartford were in a panic. The townspeople built barricades and stockpiled weapons, powder, and shot. Though most of these settlements had not been raided, rumors had King Philip and his band of cutthroats lurking everywhere, ready to strike. Metacom had been right. The colonists no longer laughed when they heard the name King Philip.

The English troops continued their vigil at Montaup. Metacom would have to leave the swamp soon and return home, they thought. When he did, they would welcome him with a hail of lead. The English believed that by killing Metacom they would cut out the heart of the Indian uprising. All they had to do, they felt, was wait him out.

Meanwhile, on July 29, nearly a month after Metacom fled from Montaup with his people, Cudworth led a large band of his troops to Dartmouth. The people in that battered town were still jittery after the Wampanoags' raid. It was hoped the sight of soldiers would buoy their spirits.

There was one problem. Most of the Massachusetts troops had already gone home. If Cudworth left, there would only be a few dozen men at Montaup to watch for Metacom. However, a patrol of Rhode Island boats was due. Cudworth left for Dartmouth, sure that his fort was well covered.

Shortly after Cudworth and his men rode south, however, the Wampanoags stole north under cover of darkness along the eastern shore of the Taunton River. Many carried lightweight birchbark canoes over their heads.

Several miles upriver, the Indians slid their canoes into the river and paddled across. Leaving the swamp behind, the Indians hid their canoes in the tall grass by the river and began the long night's march.

Metacom scanned the ranks of his marching people. They stretched back farther than he could see in the dark night. His warriors marched near the front, muskets slung over their shoulders. But most of the line was made up of women, little children, and men too old to fight.

Metacom wheeled and looked ahead. There, shrouded in darkness, lay the Rehoboth plain. They would march all night and try to cross the open plain before daybreak. A daytime crossing would be too risky. They might be seen. Metacom could not risk a battle with the colonists as long as women and children were in his ranks.

16

Escape

Captain Daniel Henchman of Boston, shirtless and sweaty in the hot sun, lifted the heavy rocks and placed them on the rising wall of the fort at Montaup, or Mount Hope, as the English called it. The fort would give the English a strong position. From here they would be able to command this territory for years to come. There would be no more uprisings in Wampanoag country, the captain thought, mopping his sweaty brow.

Henchman and his men worked happily. They considered themselves lucky. King Philip would come slithering out of the swamp any day now, starving and ready to surrender. Henchman and his men would be heroes back home. They might be awarded parcels of the Wampanoags' valuable land. They might even get a little rich for their trouble.

After sundown, Henchman walked along the shore where the lookouts were posted. There had been no sign of Indians for days. "Keep a sharp eye, men," Henchman barked. He expected the Indians to try to sneak into Montaup, looking for food. He wanted to be ready.

"Sir, a boat heading this way," a lookout announced. A trading boat slid up to the bank. Two men in officer's uniforms climbed down. They walked up the beach to Henchman and saluted. The looks on their faces were grim.

"Why so gloomy, men?" Henchman asked, returning the salute.

"Sir, King Philip has been seen crossing the Rehoboth plain with a large body of people," one of the young officers said.

Henchman's face went pale. He looked across the water at the misty bog, where he had imagined 1,000 Indians would emerge and surrender at any hour. Well, there were no Indians there. They had gone. King Philip had escaped. Henchman tried to keep his composure.

Meanwhile, Plymouth Governor Josiah Winslow slammed his fist down hard on his desk when a young messenger brought him the news of King Philip's movements. "Escaped," Winslow raged, "how?"

The governor paced back and forth in his office. He was furious with Colonel Cudworth, the commander of the Plymouth forces, for not going after the Wampanoags more aggressively. First he had allowed them to escape the peninsula. Now he had let them slip through his grasp at the Pocasset swamps. If the army had stopped King Philip's forces in either of these places, the so-called Indian rebellion would have been ended. But now the Wampanoags were free. They had reached the mainland and

were heading for central Massachusetts, home of the Nipmuck Indians.

The Nipmucks had been friends of the Wampanoags since before the days of Massasoit. They were now among the largest and strongest tribes in New England. If King Philip could persuade them to join his cause, the colonies might really have a mess on their hands.

Metacom had visited the Nipmucks again and again to enlist them in his war. Even while the Wampanoags were pinned down in the swamp, Metacom sent agents to the Nipmucks. They showed off things Wampanoag raiders were stealing from abandoned farmhouses—the clothing, guns, and money that could be had for the taking in wartime. Metacom wanted the Nipmucks to know that they weren't only fighting for a principle.

Metacom's strategy seemed to work. A vocal and violent war faction emerged within the Nipmucks. The tribe was still officially at peace with the colonies. But the Nipmuck war faction acted anyway. Led by a man named Matoonas, they rode into the Massachusetts village of Mendon and killed several settlers. One thing really bothered Massachusetts about Matoonas' raid. He and his braves were from a praying Indian town. If even those loyal Indians would turn against the colonists, where would it all end?

Massachusetts had never seen such violence on the part of its Indians. Now that the Wampanoags were on the loose in the Bay Colony to spread their gospel of war on the white man, panic spread from Boston all the way to distant Westfield.

Meanwhile, bands of armed colonists from Providence, Rehoboth, and Taunton headed for a face-off with the fleeing King Philip. Marching with them was a well-armed party of Mohegans, the Connecticut Indians who had long been close friends with the colonists—a little too close, some Indians felt. The Mohegans were an aggressive, violent people, mistrusted by many Indians. They felt the Mohegans were no more than ruthless mercenaries and henchmen for the colonists.

The colonial troops and their Mohegan allies made camp in a forest near the Rehoboth plain. King Philip's camp was close by.

Some Mohegans went ahead to scout. When they crept close to the Wampanoag camp, they were amazed at the numbers of women and children there. There were far more of them than warriors. Philip seemed to be much weaker than anyone thought. When the excited Mohegans finished their report, the colonists drew up plans for what they thought would be the final battle with the Wampanoags.

Just before dawn Metacom was awakened by the sound of Mohegan war whoops. They came from Weetamo's campsite, where the women and children slept. Metacom leaped up.

Many of his tired warriors were already running toward the source of the noise.

The men arrived to see Weetamo's people fleeing from the colonists' bullets, while the Mohegans mowed through the campsite, firing guns and slashing with their swords. Metacom's warriors hid behind rocks and trees and tried to make a stand, but they had been caught completely by surprise. Many of Metacom's best fighters were slain, including Nimrod, one of his chief counselors. Metacom found Nimrod face down in the dirt, a war hatchet buried in his back. Anguished, Metacom saw that retreat was the only way. He fled with his people, leaving their camp and everything they owned in the world abandoned on the rocky plain.

Metacom led the fleeing people into a swamp. They expected the colonists to come quickly after them. Metacom's heart sank. He feared he would have to surrender. His men were poorly armed. Many had to leave ammunition and even guns behind. To make things worse, their stores of food and plunder were also back in the campsite.

But this fact actually saved the Wampanoags. When they fled their camp, the mercenary Mohegans dug right into the booty they left behind. The Mohegans got so immersed that they forgot about the Wampanoags. Long into the afternoon, the Mohegans were still poking and sorting through their war loot.

The colonial forces were in no mood for a swamp fight without the help of the Mohegans. They decided to wait. That afternoon, Captain Henchman arrived with his troops. The captain was no more eager to plunge into the bog after Philip than the others.

Meanwhile, Metacom stood in the muck at the edge of the

swamp with Unkompoin. Where were the English? Metacom had expected them to press the attack. But there wasn't a soldier in sight. Metacom and his uncle peered across the plain, where smoke rose from a fire in the colonists' camp. It appeared that, rather than preparing to attack, the colonial troops were preparing dinner.

Henchman and the other commanders had decided to wait until morning to attack the swamp. They had no taste for it in any case. Many of them secretly hoped King Philip and his people would flee in the dark of night, making the whole battle unnecessary. After all, they reasoned, the Wampanoags were beaten. They had few warriors, no food or belongings, and were far from home. Let them flee to the hills. Then the colonies could have their land and be spared the trouble of dealing with them.

Next morning, when Henchman and his troops found the Wampanoags had gone, they could hardly have been surprised. Henchman probably looked at the rolling green hills to the west and imagined the limping Wampanoags swallowed up in them. What harm could they possibly do now?

17

Our Indians Are Friendly

In 1675, the town of Springfield, in western Massachusetts, had good reason to feel proud of itself. Its population of over 500 people made it the largest of the many settlements running up and down the Connecticut River. The town had a church, a schoolhouse, and some of the finest-looking homes and shops in the area.

Springfield had something else—good relations with the local Indians who lived a mile or so down the road in a barricaded camp. Their chief, Wequogan, was often in town to buy things for himself and his people. Old Wequogan would never allow any trouble, the townspeople said. Springfield didn't have to worry about Indian trouble.

Of late, Indian trouble had been the rule in outlying towns like Springfield. Without warning, squads of Indians would burst out of the forest with loud war whoops, shooting people in their fields or on the streets, looting and torching the houses. Indian raiders swept through the small wilderness settlements of Massachusetts and Connecticut, leaving a trail of dead bodies and burning buildings in their wake.

The new wave of terror began after the Wampanoags escaped from the swamp outside Rehoboth in July. By October half the towns of western Massachusetts had to be evacuated to keep the citizens safe. But not Springfield. They didn't have to worry about their Indians joining the Wampanoags or Nipmucks. Their Indians were friendly.

One day in early October, Springfield's soldiers rode off to the nearby town of Hadley, where hostile Indians had been sighted. While the troops were away, a report reached Springfield that the local Indians down the road had Wampanoags in their fort—infamous houseguests, to be sure.

Springfield's authorities relayed the new report to their troops, but most people didn't believe it. Not *their* Indians. They were too friendly to harbor bloodthirsty savages. The town decided to stock and barricade the garrison house just the same, since so many towns had been attacked.

The next morning, Lieutenant Thomas Cooper and the local constable rode on horseback out to the Indian fort to take a look around. Cooper had a lot of faith in the local Indians. Mainly he wanted to show the constable, and the rest of the town, how silly those Wampanoag rumors were.

Before they reached the fort, the men came upon a pair of Indian men standing in the road, holding rifles. "Strange," said Cooper, "Wequogan doesn't usually post sentries . . ."

Suddenly the Indians lifted their rifles and fired. The constable was hit in the face. He tumbled off the back of his horse into the high grass, dead. Cooper turned to run. The Indians fired again and hit Cooper in the back. Cooper felt faint from the pain of his wound. But he gritted his teeth and gripped his saddle horn tightly. He had to get back and warn the others.

Cooper galloped into town, barely clinging to his horse, and warned the shocked people of Springfield with his dying gasps. They rang the church bell, the signal to flee to the garrison. Then, in minutes, the Indians were upon them.

The Indians poured into town, shouting and shooting flaming arrows into the abandoned houses and barns, killing horses, pigs, and sheep. Leading the way was old Wequogan himself, barking orders to his men.

The attack went on for many hours. Dozens of houses were set afire. Black plumes of smoke filled the sky and could be seen from miles away. Most of the people had reached the garrison before the attack started. Only one woman was killed. But more than a third of the people of Springfield lost their homes to the hungry flames. When the soldiers finally returned from Hadley, they could do little but watch helplessly as their town went up in flames. The Indians had fled.

The Wampanoags headed for Quabog, in central Massachusetts, home of the Nipmucks. They had been staying there with the Nipmucks since July when they escaped from the swamp. In old days, the Nipmucks paid tribute to the Wampanoag's sachem, Massasoit. Over the years the two tribes had stayed close.

The Nipmucks greeted the weary Wampanoags with dancing and feasting. The presence of the vengence-hungry Metacom ignited the war faction of the Nipmucks, which won out over the old peace chiefs. Together, the two tribes began a series of raids on the wilderness towns of western Massachusetts and Connecticut. The Nipmucks were the larger tribe and most of the attacks were led by their war chiefs, Matoonas, Monoco,

Shoshanim, and Muttaump. But inspiration for the war came from Metacom. His goal to drive the white men back across the sea echoed in the hearts of many Indians. Almost everywhere the raiders went they found local Indians, such as Wequogan and his band, ready and willing to help.

The colonial troops were in a dilemma. Indian bands were hiding in the thick woodlands at the center of the colony, coming out to ambush a town, then disappearing again into the forest. No one knew their hideouts, much less where or when they would strike next. If the troops split up to guard each of the towns, the Indians were left unopposed in the forest, free to plan and carry out new raids. If the soldiers chose to combine their forces and track the Indians, the towns would be left unguarded and vulnerable.

The people in the wilderness settlements now lived in constant fear of Indian attacks. After hearing so many reports of farmers massacred in their fields by waves of Indian raiders springing from the quiet forest, the people became too nervous to work in their own fields. Large farms, once productive, now lay idle and barren, and many towns suffered food shortages.

Finally, it was decided to evacuate several of the smaller wilderness towns to allow the armies to protect the larger settlements. The new ghost towns were often sacked, looted, and burned by scavenging Indians, out for plunder.

The raids continued until November brought colder weather and a lull in the fighting. Had the Indians gone to their winter campgrounds to wait out the bitter cold? Nevertheless, the colonists kept wary eyes on the trails to the vast forests. As the quiet snows of winter blanketed the Northeast, New England was in something of a state of shock.

During the winter Metacom took his chief war captains and several braves on a trip to visit the fierce Mohawk tribe in

upstate New York. Metacom and his men didn't have to worry these days about taking care of their women, children, and elderly. Weetamo had taken them to Narragansett country, where Awashonks and her people had gone before. Now Metacom and his warriors were free to roam at will. They planned to spend the winter months forging new alliances with Indian bands.

After a long hike through the snow-covered forests, Metacom and his men spent many days sitting before the council fires of the Mohawks, talking with their war chiefs. The Mohawks were the best warriors in the Northeast. If Metacom could now persuade them to join the Indians of New England in the war, they would have a good chance of defeating the colonists, who were still reeling from the autumn raids.

But the Mohawks were not anxious to fight the white men. Their relations with the authorities in New York were good. The chiefs folded their arms and scowled when Metacom tried to reason with them.

"The men of Plymouth were like brothers to us in old times," Metacom said. "But white men must always conquer their brothers, that is their way," he warned. "One day, what has happened to us will happen to you. They will take your land and force you to wander in the wilderness."

The Mohawks were insulted to be told how to run their affairs by such a young chief. Besides, they didn't trust anyone who was friendly with the Nipmucks. The Mohawks had made war against the Nipmucks recently, and they hadn't forgotten all their old grudges.

Metacom decided he would rather face the blizzards in the forests than the chilly attitudes of the Mohawk chiefs. He and his men left quietly early one morning for the long hike back on the snow-covered northern trail. As Metacom walked mile after mile on the hard, frozen ground, his deep brown eyes were full of sadness. He had come to make allies, but he had made enemies instead.

Meanwhile, Weetamo, Awashonks, and the rest of the Wampanoags had made camp near the Narragansett villages. The people were glad to have this peaceful woodland refuge so near to their own homes, even if it meant living among their old enemies.

The Narragansetts had often turned down requests from Metacom to join in his war. They preferred a profitable peace with the colonies. However, they agreed to give shelter to the Wampanoag women and children. Still, they may have had selfish motives. After all, they had little faith in Metacom's cause. They thought from the start the Wampanoags would be badly beaten. If that happened, the Narragansetts would grow stronger by adding Wampanoag women and children to their numbers.

Already, one of the Narragansetts' war chiefs, Quinnapin, had taken a Wampanoag wife. He married Weetamo herself, sachem of the Pocassets, whose late husband was also a chief, the ill-fated Wamsutta.

The Narragansetts seemed to like having the refugee Wampanoags among them. However, there was one problem. The colonists were furious about it. The Narragansetts had made a promise to the colonies not to shelter any Wampanoags. The colonists were worried, lest the angry rebels from Montaup spread their war fever to other Indians.

The Narragansetts had agreed to turn over any Wampanoags who sought shelter with them. But they didn't think the agreement included civilian refugees. Surely the women and children were harmless, the Narragansetts thought. Even the white men could see that.

But the colonies stuck to their conditions. In October they summoned the Narragansett sachem, Canonchet, to Boston for a conference. The chief agreed to give up the Wampanoags in ten days. But the ten days passed and the Wampanoags were not surrendered.

Canonchet was in a terrible dilemma. He didn't wish to antagonize the colonists. But to turn over innocent Wampanoag women and children, only to be sold into slavery, just didn't seem right.

18

"Many Were Terribly Barbecued"

O ver 1,000 heavily armed men trudged through the slanting December snow toward Narragansett country. They were part of the army of the United Colonies, the largest force ever assembled in New England. Their mission: "destroy" the Narragansetts.

No one seemed to think it odd to be attacking the Narragansetts, who were at peace with the colonies. No one seemed to think it odd that this huge army was not marching after King Philip and his Indians, who had been burning, looting, and killing for months, and were last sighted far to the north, in the opposite direction.

Perhaps the reason no one questioned these things is that attacking the Narragansetts was likely to be easier than attacking the wily King Philip, and certainly much more profitable. Not only did the colonists know where to find these Indians, but in return for "destroying" them the soldiers were to receive grants of Narragansett land, said to be the finest in New England. Such land would be worth a great deal of money.

While on the march, the army captured an Indian named Peter and threatened to hang him unless he showed the way to the Narragansetts' hidden fort. The nervous Peter led the troops through the frozen marshland.

The march had begun at five that morning. At noon Peter pointed out their target, an island in the midst of a swamp. The island was surrounded by a manmade mound of dirt topped off with a tangle of trees. Blockhouses stood at many points along the built-up barrier.

The island was a fortress. On it stood some 500 Indian wigwams, housing over 3,000 Narragansetts. Forewarned, the Indians crouched down inside, quietly watching and waiting for the invasion they knew would come.

Peter showed the soldiers to a breach in the palisade. There, between two blockhouses was an opening barred by a single log five feet off the ground.

Two men rushed to the opening. One was shot and killed as he reached the log. The other got inside, but was quickly gunned down. The Indians had the opening well covered. They were ready for a fight.

Next the troops rushed the opening in waves. Many were cut down, but their numbers were so great that they soon broke through and the battle spilled into the settlement.

Inside, fighting went from wigwam to wigwam, but Indian riflemen poured shot on the troops, and the army suffered heavy casualties. But the battle turned when the soldiers lit torches and lobbed them atop the wigwams. A roaring blaze and a

cloud of thick black smoke swallowed the settlement. Indians in the flaming wigwams, mostly women and children, had to choose between burning to death or facing the soldiers' bullets. One colonist reported, "Many were terribly barbecued."

Others ran screaming from their wigwams. Men, women, even little children, were stabbed or shot at point-blank range by the soldiers bent on massacre. Canonchet, who was leading the Indians, saw his people were in danger of being wiped out. He retreated with survivors into the woods, forced to leave many wounded behind, as well as all the town's food and supplies. Over 600 Indians died in the long battle, mostly women and children. The colonists reported fifty of their own dead, but it might well have been many more.

The colonists had been after the Narragansetts' land. They had also been worried that the Narragansetts might enter the war on King Philip's side. After this battle, known to colonists as the Great Swamp Fight, the land belonged to the settlers. But they failed to utterly "destroy" the Narragansetts. Nothing would keep the survivors out of the war now.

As the colonies celebrated victory, the Narragansetts plotted vengeance. Most of their survivors, some 300 men, were warriors, now without wives and families. These men, in their moment of blackest despair, felt they had nothing left to lose.

Canonchet led his angry warriors on a hard march across the frozen marshlands to the hilly forests of central Massachusetts. There he hoped to find Metacom, and to join his cause. In many ways, Metacom's war seemed more their cause now than his.

The colonial troops disbanded and went home after the Great Swamp Fight. They thought the danger was over. But the Narragansetts had other ideas.

Meanwhile, in Quabog, at the Nipmucks' camp, a runner had just come with word from Metacom. The Mohawks would not join the fighting. The mood in the Indian camp was downcast. They knew they would need more warriors to carry on their struggle. They were very near despair over finding any.

When Nipmuck sentries saw the Narragansetts coming over the rise, they opened fire. It was believed the Narragansetts were allied with the colonists.

The Narragansetts backed off and sent envoys into the Nipmuck camp bearing an offering of peace and friendship— the severed heads of a dozen Englishmen.

The Nipmucks greeted their southern brethren with dancing and feasting. They were no longer saddened over the Mohawks' refusal to join the war. The Narragansetts were warriors to be reckoned with even in normal times, and now they were doubly fierce. Haunted by memories of what the English had done to their women and children at the Great Swamp Fight, they were ready for a battle.

19
"Help Us, Lord, or We Perish"

The colonists felt more comfortable after the Great Swamp Fight than they had in a long time. They knew hundreds of Narragansett warriors had joined the revolt, but the colonists also had to tend to spring planting. Farmers turned soldiers had neglected their crops last season. Now it was time for soldiers to turn back to farming. The Indians could be dealt with after new seeds were sewn.

Still Massachusetts people were uneasy about the hostile Indians on the frontier. As a precaution, the colony's leaders sent two friendly praying Indians, Job Kattenanit and James Quannapohit, to spy on the Indian camps.

Quannapohit returned on January 24, 1676, with a full report. Among other things, the Indian said that the town of Lancaster would be attacked in three weeks. The Massachusetts authorities thanked the loyal Indian spy and filed his report in a drawer. For reasons of their own, they did not warn the people of Lancaster. Perhaps they didn't believe their own agent. Colonists never had much faith in the word of an Indian.

Along with the Narragansetts, the Indians now had the help of Weetamo and her Pocassets and Awashonks with her Sakonets. The Indians were quick to flex their new muscle. Beginning in February, they swept through the settlements, leaving a trail of charred homes and mutilated corpses, and disappearing again into the forest, where the colonists dared not follow.

On the night of February 9, Job Kattenanit, out of breath from a long run, pounded on the door of an English soldier in Cambridge. "They come, they come," the excited Indian said. Four hundred Indians were marching on Lancaster.

This time the Indian's warning was heeded. In the middle of the night, soldiers in nearby towns were rousted from their beds and called to defend Lancaster. But by the time the first troops arrived after dawn, billowing black smoke was rising from the many houses already ablaze, and the sky crackled with the sound of musket fire.

The Indians had already burned down most of the abandoned houses in town. They also broke down a wall at one of the garrisons where the townspeople were sheltered, making off with over twenty prisoners. The troops eventually drove the Indians away, but not before Lancaster had suffered terribly. More than fifty townspeople died that morning. The town was deserted by its frightened people one week later.

Ten days after the raid at Lancaster, Indians stole into the town of Medfield at dawn. Before the sleepy townspeople knew what happened, the Indians had set some fifty buildings afire.

Soldiers garrisoned in the town forced the Indians to retreat, but not until several persons were killed and the town nearly destroyed.

The raids went on and on. Corpses littered the streets and buildings blazed in Groton, Marlborough, Andover, Billerica, Chelmsford, and Woburn. Just south of the capital in Boston, raiders fell on Braintree, Weymouth, and Scituate. These towns had assumed they were safely out of danger, since the fighting had been confined to the outlying settlements. But now no one seemed safe. Even the people of Boston grew wary.

Indians seemed to be everywhere. The allied bands fought in separate raiding parties. Canonchet and the Narragansetts swarmed on Warwick and Wickford near their old territory, and burned down eighty houses in Providence. Matoonas and the Nipmuck sachems terrorized the mid-colony settlements. Metacom led his newly strengthened Wampanoags back to the place where it all started, raiding Bridgewater and Rehoboth in Plymouth Colony; and on March 26 they killed forty-two men just five miles north of Plymouth itself.

The New England colonies were reeling. For a time it seemed as if Metacom's plan to drive the white men back across the sea from whence they came might come to pass. Still the colonists saw the causes of the war not in their treatment of the Indians but in their behavior toward God. Many colonists felt their sins offended God so much that ". . . instead of turning His hand against (the Indians), the Lord feeds and nourishes them up to be a scourge to the whole land."

The colonists turned to God in their despair. They spent days praying in meeting houses throughout the colonies. Sorrowful, war-weary colonists beat their breasts and humbly begged God's forgiveness: "Help us, Lord, or we perish," cried one, quoting the Bible.

While the colonists sent prayers to heaven, they got help from an unexpected source right here on earth—the Indians themselves.

When the war broke out, many Indians in the praying towns turned against the colonies and joined the raiders. Other praying Indians remained loyal, but the colonists had a hard time trusting them. Though the praying Indians' knowledge of the enemy's habits and methods would be useful, it was felt they, too, would turn traitors when pressured by their people. But now that the war's tide had turned, the colonies reluctantly asked these loyal Indians for help.

Meanwhile, other Indian groups helped the colonists win one of the great prizes of the war. In April a search party of Connecticut troops, with the help of Mohegan and Pequot scouts, corraled Canonchet himself. The war chief was gathering food in his former hometown when Indian scouts tracked him down and captured him. Canonchet was taken to Stonington and brutally executed. The Indians cut off his head and slashed his body into four pieces. Connecticut troops burned the remains, except the chief's head. They sent that gory trophy to the council at Hartford.

In mid-April, Metacom met with the chiefs of all the allied tribes. To many of them, the death of Canonchet, one of their boldest warriors, was a bad omen. Medicine men, or powwows, were summoned by the chiefs to placate the spirits.

The powwows donned masks carved with animal faces, meant to scare off evil spirits, and danced around the campfire chanting in low, mournful tones. The grim-faced chiefs sat in stony silence until the song ended. Then Metacom lit his pipe, blew a blast of smoke, and passed the pipe around the circle of sachems. "The English are a wounded animal," he said. "Their painful cries echo in the forest. We must move quickly, before they have time to bind their sores. We must unite and take the main road to Boston—their heart and soul."

Metacom wished to combine the strength of all the tribes into one powerful army and march on Boston. He felt the white capital could be taken by the 15th of May, just one month away. Some of the other chiefs favored sticking with their current strategy of sending small bands on quick hit-and-run raids. Such raids had kept the colonists off balance. They weren't able to gather their vast forces in one place, for the Indians had been everywhere. If the Indians banded together, the white men would too. Since the white men's numbers were far greater, such a face-off could be disastrous.

When the discussion was over, the plans were put to a vote. The young warriors whooped and howled to signal support for Metacom's strategy, which was adopted in spite of the frowns of the other chiefs. The young men hungered for a showdown with the colonial army. They had tasted success against the hated enemy. They now wanted to move in for the kill.

The town of Sudbury sat at the end of the main road to Boston, on the east bank of the Sudbury River. Before dawn on April 21 the newly united Indian forces swarmed the settlement. Once again they took the complacent colonists by surprise. While the colonists ran for cover in their garrisons, the Indians set fire to the homes they left behind.

The nearby towns of Concord and Waterton saw the rising plumes of black smoke from Sudbury and had no doubt of their source. Soldiers quickly mounted their horses to relieve the beseiged settlement, and messengers were sent to other towns for more troops.

Soon a large force of fighting men arrived to battle the Indians. Both sides fought fiercely, but the well-armed and mounted colonists drove the Indians back across the river.

As the battle moved away from the settlement, the Indians employed a clever strategy. A small band retreated into the hills. They were quickly pursued by a larger squad of about sixty colonists. But when the colonists emerged over the hill, they found themselves engulfed by hundreds of warriors. Over half the squad was wiped out. The rest mounted a nearby hill and dug in to do battle for their lives.

The fighting raged until evening, when the Indians retreated. They had fought fiercely, inflicting perhaps the heaviest losses yet on the white men, who suffered over seventy deaths. But the Indians' losses were even greater. As many as 120 warriors were killed.

To the white men, unused to so many deaths, this seemed like an Indian victory. But to the Indians, who were aiming beyond Sudbury at Boston, this must have tasted like defeat. They had thrown everything they had at the colonists, only to be pushed back across the river, and to suffer more losses than the white men.

To add insult to injury, when the battle was over, a group of shadowy figures braved the dark night to count the bodies and bury the colonists' dead. Metacom's scouts watched in disbelief as these people dug holes to bury the corpses of the hated enemy. As far as Metacom's scouts were concerned, these were no ordinary gravediggers. They were a squad of praying Indians painted for war—war against the Indians.

20

"A Doleful, Great, Naked, Dirty Beast"

The mood of the Indians turned sour after Sudbury. They had entered the battle with soaring spirits, thinking it the first step on the road to Boston and possible victory. Now they understood that victory, if it could be won at all, lay at the end of a much longer road, and would demand even greater sacrifices than they had already made.

Many Indians had spent nearly a year away from homes and farms, with little food and few comforts. Before Sudbury, most thought it had all been worth it. Scores of charred English homes and deserted English farms, hundreds of newly dug English graves, attested to the strength and will of the Indians.

But it hadn't been enough. The colonies were hurt, but they fought back harder than ever. If the

Indians killed fifty men, the colonists would regroup and oppose them with a force of 250. There was no getting to the end of them. The Indians weighed the new costs of the long, long struggle that lay ahead.

The Indians had shown great skill just staying alive for those many months, especially when food was dangerously short in their war camps. One Puritan hostage wrote about the Indians' talents for coaxing food from the wilderness:

> *They would pick up old bones, and cut them to pieces at the joints, and if they were full of worms and maggots, they would scald them over the fire to make the vermin come out, and then boil them, and drink up the liquor (liquid), and then beat the great ends of them in a mortar, and so eat them. They would eat horse's guts, ears, and all sorts of wild birds which they could catch: also bear, venison, beaver, tortoise, frogs, squirrels, dogs, skunks, rattlesnakes; yea, the very bark of trees . .*

Though Indians could survive on such fare for a long time, it was not the sort of life they enjoyed. After Sudbury, a good many Indians decided they had made enough sacrifices for a while. They wished to disappear back into the forest, plant crops, hunt and fish, and enjoy good home-cooked meals and the comforts of life again, to renew their fighting strength.

So, after Sudbury, groups of Indians split off from the main war parties to return to the forest to plant and gather food. Others maintained war parties and continued to raid the white settlements. But the settlers were at peak fighting strength, their troops united by the recent Indian offensives. The colonists also had many Indians loyal to them in the field. Now the newly splintered groups of Indians were very vulnerable indeed.

A group of several hundred Indians made camp at Peskeompscut, on the banks of the Connecticut River, just above a waterfall. There was no colonial army in the field anywhere near them, so the people felt safe. They took large catches of fish in the river, planted crops, and hunted in the nearby forests. From time to time, small bands of them went to Deerfield to the south and stole cattle from the white settlers, who were still laying low after earlier Indians attacks.

The settlers had no army nearby to protect them. One morning, though, a band of young volunteers mounted up for the ride to Peskeompscut. Reports said the Indians at the camp were mainly women and children. That was fine with these inexperienced soldiers. The more helpless the prey, the better.

The Indians felt so secure in their camp that they didn't even post sentries at night. So, early one morning in mid-May, the volunteers stole into the camp unnoticed and surrounded the wigwams. Just after first light, they opened fire.

Screams of agony pierced the quiet morning as the men's muskets found their marks. Men, women, and children ran from the wigwams and were cut down before they could go a few steps. Many plunged into the river to escape. The volunteers lined the banks and poured shot into the desperately swimming horde. Most of those who escaped the bullets were swept over the steep falls, their lives dashed out on the rocks below.

Hundreds of Indians, mostly women and children, were massacred that May morning at Peskeompscut. Similar scenes of tragedy, though not always so devastating, often befell the Indians in the months ahead. The colonists, sensing the weakening of the Indians' will, eagerly tracked them down in their forest bivouacs, often with the aid of talented Indian scouts from the praying Indians or other loyal bands. Tired of war to begin with, the Indians now sank into despair. Many blamed Metacom and "his" war for their misfortune. Convinced that their cause was doomed, these Indians deserted the ranks of the

Chief Massasoit's pipe

rebels and sought sanctuary from the white men.

Among the deserters was Awashonks. With her party of Sakonnets, the squaw sachem surrendered to Benjamin Church at Plymouth Colony in June. Awashonks added treachery to her plot. She promised to aid in the capture of Metacom, her own chief, to gain good treatment for her people. "We will fight for you, and will help you to Metacom's head before the Indian corn is ripe," she said. Church happily accepted the terms.

In Boston, a few days later, Sagamore John marched his war chief, Matoonas, into the city at the point of a gun. With them were 180 former fighting men, ready to throw themselves on the mercy of the colonists. To prove their sincerity, Sagamore John tied Matoonas to a tree in a public square in Boston, where he and his men shot the chief dead.

A downcast Metacom sensed the end was near. With a loyal core of followers, he traveled back toward his home country. In mid-July, the Sakonnets led Church and his men to Metacom's camp and helped ambush the Wampanoags. Metacom managed to escape, but over 100 Wampanoags were killed, and almost as many were taken prisoner, including Metacom's wife and young son. Among the dead was Unkompoin, Metacom's uncle and war chief, and Weetamo, his beloved sister-in-law.

Metacom, much grieved by the loss of those closest to him, now went with a small band back to Montaup. He wished to walk on the sacred ground of his people once again before he died. Still he would not give up. When one of his men suggested surrender, Metacom rashly ordered him killed. The victim's brother, a man named Alderman, then fled the camp, swearing to take revenge on the young chief.

Montaup was deserted; the soldiers had left months ago. Metacom wandered among the empty wigwams trying to make peace with his tortured thoughts. The great war—his great war—was over. Though scattered bands of Indians still raided, and would go on raiding for months, the English had won. In the past the English had always cheated and taken advantage of his people. Now they would do so with blood vengeance in their hearts. His people would suffer more than ever. Had the war been worth it, if this was to be its only result?

No one knows if Metacom had the time to grapple with these thoughts. On the night of August 12, Alderman, true to his vow, led Church and a band of volunteers to Metacom's shabby campsite. There were no guards posted. The volunteers surrounded the camp and began firing. Metacom's men tried to flee, but most were cut down as they ran.

Alderman himself aimed his musket at a dark figure who was running straight at him. He fired and the running man fell face down in the mud. Alderman crept up to the man and lifted his face from the mire. It was Metacom. The young chief was dead, two bullets lodged below his heart.

Alderman shouted news of his kill to the other volunteers, who laughed and whistled for sheer joy. Church, too, was jubilant. He had tracked the cunning King Philip for many weeks. Church stood over the corpse of his dead rival, fascinated with his first glimpse of the man who lit the torch that singed all New England. To Church, Metacom seemed "a doleful, great, naked, dirty beast," sprawled in the mud at Montaup.

Church quickly ordered Metacom's head cut off, his body quartered and burned. Church brought the head to Plymouth, where the gory souvenir was screwed atop a pole and left on display for twenty-five years.

After the war, several groups of Indians, mostly those in the praying towns, were allowed to live in the Bay Colony in peace almost as before. However, they now required a license if they went abroad in the forest to hunt. Most of the war-ravaged groups of Indians died out within a couple of generations. But some tribes still survive. There are more than 1,000 Wampanoag Indians living in southeastern Massachusetts today.

As for the lands of the defeated Indians, most of them were confiscated by the conquering colonies. In many cases they were used to pay the troops for their service in the war.

Hundreds of other Indians, including the wife and son of Metacom, were sold into brutal slavery in the West Indies after the war. Some colonists, including Benjamin Church, objected to this harsh treatment, for among the Indians sold into bondage were many who had remained at peace.

King Philip's war began as a feud between the Wampanoags and Plymouth Colony. It quickly spread, as Indians throughout New England sympathized with the Wampanoags' cause. The huge conflict even attracted the attention of the king of England once again to his colonies. Near the close of the war, the king sent Edward Randolph to New England to assess the situation.

Late one afternoon, Randolph sat at a small desk in his Boston inn. The king's man had little love for New England's religious reformers, so it was with a certain relish that he dipped his quill pen into the inkbottle and scratched out his report to the king about the war:

> . . . *The Indians were never civilly treated by the government, who made it their business to encroach on the Indian lands, and by degrees to drive them out. That was the ground and beginning of the late war.*

Within twenty years, the king ended the great experiments of the religious zealots of New England. Plymouth Colony was merged with Massachusetts, and the new colony was given a revised charter that made no mention of religious "missions."

The king also appointed royal governors to rule each of his colonies for him. He wanted no more nonsense.

Ironically, about one hundred years later, Americans began to feel as if the English were closing in on their freedom, just as Metacom and the Wampanoags felt about Englishmen in their day. In 1776 Americans also fought a war with the English, the American Revolutionary War, out of which the United States of America was born. The men who fought so bravely for their independence in 1776 were great-grandsons of the men who killed King Philip for seeking his.

Suggested Reading

Averill, Ester. *King Philip: The Indian Chief.* New York: Harper & Brothers, Publishers, 1950.

Hall-Quest, Olga. *Flames Over New England: The Story of King Philip's War, 1675–1676.* New York: E. P. Dutton & Company, Inc., 1967.

Josephy, Alvin M., Jr. *The Patriot Chiefs.* New York: Viking Press, 1961.

Rich, Louise Dickinson. *King Philip's War, 1675–76.* New York: Franklin Watts, Inc., 1972.

Stember, Sol. *Heroes of the American Indians.* New York: Fleet Press Corporation, 1971.

ADVANCED READING

Jennings, Francis. *The Invasion of America.* New York: W. W. Norton & Company, 1976.

Leach, Douglas. *Flintlock and Tomahawk.* New York: Macmillan Publishing Co., 1959.